TRUNK ROADS, ENGLAND
INTO THE 1990s

Prepared by Road Programme and Resources Division, The Department of Transport

LONDON: HMSO

© Crown copyright 1990
First Published 1990
Second impression 1990

ISBN 0 11 550952 6

Cover Photograph
M6 Cumbria

FOREWORD BY
THE SECRETARY OF STATE FOR TRANSPORT

My aim is to achieve a balance between the various forms of transport so that each of them can make its proper contribution to a safer, more environment-friendly and more efficient transport system.

The public and industry have, and expect to continue to have, freedom of choice in transport. They want the opportunity for greater mobility, and with increased prosperity we as a nation are able to afford it. Investment in both roads and public transport is at record levels.

This report deals specifically with the trunk road network. Trunk roads have a key part to play because they carry so much traffic, especially long distance and vital commercial and industrial traffic. The nation wants a national road system which meets its expectations. The Government aims to provide it.

The White Paper ''Roads For Prosperity'' set out the Government's plans for an expanded trunk road construction programme. This report gives a fuller account of our continuing stewardship of the network, including its maintenance and operation. It updates the previous progress report, ''Policy for Roads in England: 1987'', and gives more detail, including detail on timing of schemes, of the projects announced in ''Roads For Prosperity''.

Road improvements must be provided in a way that promotes safety and protects the environment. This report describes how we are doing this. I place particular importance on the further measures to improve the environment which are set out in Section 5.

February 1990

CONTENTS

1 INTRODUCTION

1.1 This report describes progress with the construction, management and maintenance of the trunk road network in England since "Policy for Roads in England:1987"(Cm 125) was published in April 1987. The trunk roads are the backbone of Britain's road system. They represent only 4.4 per cent of the total mileage of roads, but carry 31 per cent of all traffic, including 54 per cent of heavy goods vehicle traffic (see Figure 1).

Responsibilities and objectives

1.2 The trunk road network in England comprises some 6,600 miles of motorways and other roads for which the Secretary of State for Transport is the highway authority. The Secretary of State's purpose is to provide, maintain and manage a network of roads to cater for through traffic. The objectives underlying trunk road building and improvement continue to be:

- to assist economic growth by reducing transport costs;

- to improve the environment by removing through traffic from unsuitable roads in towns and villages;

- to enhance road safety.

Value for money, concern for the environment and safety also determine how the network is managed and maintained.

Traffic growth

1.3 Higher economic activity and prosperity have led to a large increase in demand for transport and travel. Today there is over three times the volume of passenger transport and over twice the amount of freight transport as forty years ago. Nearly two thirds of households now have regular use of a car compared with only 14 per cent in 1951. While there has been a vast increase in the volume of travel and shifts in the modes used in the past forty years, the road system has continued to be the dominant means of inland transport. Between 1952 and 1988 road's share of passenger travel increased from 80 per cent to 93 per cent. Over the same period, goods moved (ton miles) by road have increased fourfold with the share of all goods moved inland (excluding waterborne and pipeline) nearly doubling from 46 per cent to 88 per cent. These changes have placed considerable demands on the road system and the trunk roads in particular.

1.4 New National Road Traffic Forecasts published in 1989 (Reference 1) suggest that traffic demand could increase by between 83 per cent and 142 per cent by the year 2025, compared with 1988. These forecasts are largely determined by forecasts of economic growth. They are in no sense a target or an option; they are an estimate of the increase in demand as increased prosperity brings more commercial activity and gives more people the opportunity to travel and to travel more frequently and for longer distances.

Congestion

1.5 The growth in traffic has brought problems of congestion on the trunk road network. The forecasts of traffic demand indicate that this congestion will get much worse unless action is taken. Action is necessary because congestion imposes higher costs on the consumer and reduces the competitiveness of British industry; it leads to more accidents; it encourages traffic to use unsuitable roads; and it wastes fuel, thereby increasing exhaust emissions.

Figure 1   ROAD TRAFFIC GREAT BRITAIN

TRAFFIC BY TYPE OF ROAD
(Billion Vehicle Miles)

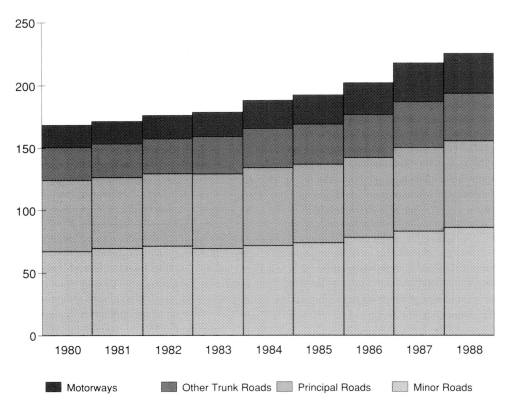

■ Motorways   ■ Other Trunk Roads   ▨ Principal Roads   □ Minor Roads

HEAVY GOODS VEHICLE TRAFFIC
By Type of Road

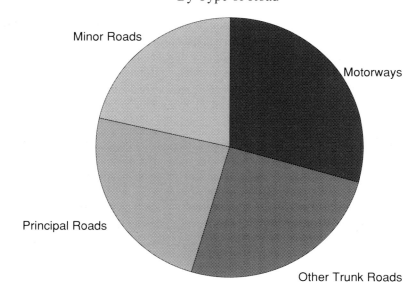

1.6   Following a review of congestion on the trunk road network, the White Paper, "Roads For Prosperity" (Cm 693) announced a doubling of the trunk road programme. The proposals in the White Paper are aimed primarily at providing extra capacity on the motorways and other strategic inter-urban routes. They are not intended to cater for all forecast demand to 2025. There will be cases where on economic or environmental grounds it is neither practicable nor desirable to meet the demand by road building, for example in city centres. Here in particular better traffic management, parking controls and improvements to public transport, including the development of new facilities such as light rail systems, can make a contribution to dealing with congestion and reducing the environmental effect of road traffic.

1.7   It has been suggested that instead of providing more roadspace the Government should seek to curb the use of cars and promote a switch from road to rail. Investment in public transport is running at very high levels and is set to rise still further. The Government will continue to support the high levels of investment needed to modernise and improve rail services. The Department is currently reviewing the scope for improvements in the Section 8 grant system for encouraging the transfer of freight to the railways. But increased investment in public transport will not solve the problems of congestion on our main inter-urban roads. The mobility, flexibility and convenience afforded by a car is greatly prized by the private motorist. Road and rail for the most part serve different markets and for most journeys one mode cannot readily be substituted for the other. Even a 50 per cent increase in rail traffic would be equivalent to only 5 per cent of present road traffic - about one year's growth in recent years.

The environment

1.8   It is important that the requirements for road travel are met in as environmentally friendly a way as possible. The emphasis of the expanded programme is to increase capacity on existing motorways and other strategic routes. This will help to minimise the requirement for additional land and the overall impact on the countryside. A great deal of effort already goes into assessing the environmental impact of potential schemes and designing them to fit as sympathetically as possible into the landscape. But with the expansion of the road programme the Government intends to do even more. New proposals to improve the environmental treatment of motorways and trunk roads are set out in Section 5 of this report.

1.9   There is also concern about the effects of forecast traffic demand on emissions of carbon dioxide, the principal greenhouse gas. The greenhouse effect is a global problem and requires concerted international action. The Government is playing a leading role in the international discussions now under way and an Environment White Paper is to be published later this year. The scope for reducing emissions from the transport sector - which accounts for some 20 per cent of Britain's carbon dioxide emissions - will be considered more fully there. But to stop further inter- urban road improvement would not stop traffic growth, since demand is largely determined by growth in the economy. Experience in urban areas and on unimproved trunk roads has shown that road users will put up with long delays, change their travel times or use less suitable routes where spare capacity still exists. And in the stop-start conditions caused by congestion, motor vehicles produce more exhaust emissions.

1.10   The best way of curbing carbon dioxide emissions from motor vehicles is to increase engine efficiency so that they consume less fuel. The average fuel efficiency of cars on Britain's roads has improved by over 20 per cent since 1978. With changes in vehicle technology an improvement of 50 per cent is achievable compared to 1978 (Reference 2). Good driving technique, regular vehicle maintenance and not using a car for very short journeys, especially when the engine is cold, can help to reduce fuel consumption. The Government is considering how best to encourage this. The Department of Transport publishes a booklet giving details of new car fuel consumption.

1.11 The Government has been successful in encouraging the use of unleaded petrol through a tax incentive. Unleaded petrol now has nearly a 30 per cent share of the petrol market. The Government is committed to introducing the provisions of recent EC Directives on emissions from vehicles. These set stringent limits on the emission from new vehicles of carbon monoxide, hydrocarbons and the oxides of nitrogen as well as imposing limits on the emission of particulates by diesel engined cars. These new standards will take effect in the early 1990s. The new limits on gaseous emissions are likely to entail the widespread use of three way catalyst technology in vehicles with petrol engines.

1.12 Tighter noise limits for new vehicles are now coming into effect as a result of an EC Directive. This will mean that the noise from some of the heaviest lorries will have been halved over the past decade.

2   FINANCING THE TRUNK ROAD NETWORK

2.1 Spending on the trunk road network in 1987/88, 1988/89 and the forecast spend in the current financial year to 31 March 1990 are summarised in the table below.

	1987/88 £m	1988/89 £m	1989/90 £m
New construction	607	707	960
Capital maintenance	264	190	337
Current maintenance	84	102	97
TOTAL	**955**	**999**	**1,394**

Expenditure (excluding VAT) increased by 10 per cent in real terms compared to the previous three-year period ending 31 March 1987.

2.2 The table below sets out planned spending on the trunk road network for the three years to 1992/93.

	1990/91 £m	1991/92 £m	1992/93 £m
New construction	1,282	1,322	1,403
Capital maintenance	412	444	448
Current maintenance	120	127	134
TOTAL	**1,814**	**1,893**	**1,985**

2.3 The Government is committed to delivering the expanded programme announced in "Roads For Prosperity" as a matter of priority. Increased financial provision has been made for the three-year period to 1992/93 for new construction. Total expenditure of £4,007 million is planned, which is an increase (excluding VAT) of 50 per cent in real terms on the three-year period ending 31 March 1990. This increase will enable a steady build up of activity on the programme. It is expected that construction of many new schemes announced in "Roads For Prosperity" will be under way by the mid 1990s with a substantial number being completed by the year 2000.

2.4 Spending on capital maintenance is also to be increased over the next three years. At £1,304 million this represents an increase of 42 per cent in real terms compared with the three-year period ending 31 March 1990. This will enable continuing progress with the major programme of bridge maintenance, and elimination of the maintenance backlogs identified in the early 1980s by 1992/93. It is also planned to spend £381 million on current maintenance, an increase of 18 per cent in real terms.

2.5 Figure 2 illustrates trends in real spending on the trunk road network in England since 1978/79.

Figure 2   ROADS VOTE EXPENDITURE £m
(1989/90 prices)

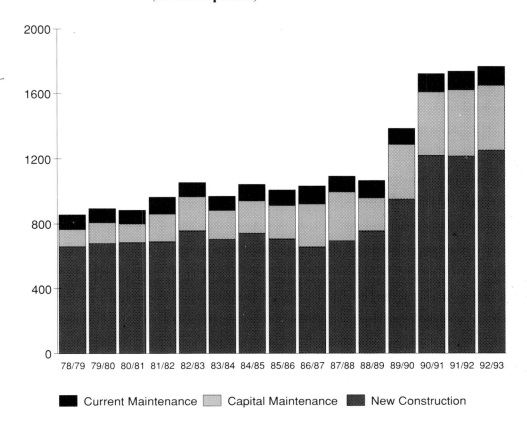

Current Maintenance ■   Capital Maintenance ▨   New Construction ▦

3   NEW CONSTRUCTION AND IMPROVEMENT

Achievements 1987-89

3.1 In the period April 1987 to 31 December 1989 83 national trunk road schemes (those costing over £1million) were completed involving construction of 289 miles of new or improved road. A full list of completions is at Table 1. They include the widening of the M25 between Junctions 11 and 13 relieving the serious congestion on this very busy part of the motorway between Chertsey and Staines on the western outskirts of London. After a long and controversial history the A30 Okehampton bypass was opened to traffic in the summer of 1988 bringing much needed relief from traffic jams for people travelling to the West Country and a more peaceful atmosphere to the town itself. The new bypass is an example of how a new road can be built in a sensitive area with the minimum of damage to the environment. Other schemes completed include the Portwood - Denton section of the M63/M66 Manchester Outer Ring Road, the A406 South Woodford to Barking Relief Road, the A1 Wetherby Bypass, the A46 Coventry Eastern Bypass, the A616 Stocksbridge - M1 Link and the dualling of the A11 between Wymondham and Cringleford on the outskirts of Norwich.

3.2 Table 2 lists 45 national schemes under construction at 1 January 1990 with a total estimated cost of nearly £1 billion. They include the remaining stages of the M40 between London and Birmingham, the A1 Newcastle Western Bypass, the A14 M1 - A1 Link Road and the missing link of the M20 between Maidstone and Ashford. The M20 and improved A20 between Folkestone and Dover will link the Channel Tunnel and the two ports to the motorway network.

3.3   Table 4 gives details of major changes in schemes included in "Policy for Roads in England: 1987". Table 5 gives details of local authority highway schemes being funded with the aid of grant under section 272 of the Highways Act 1980.

Private finance

3.4   The Dartford tunnels have become a serious bottleneck on the London Orbital Route. Following the passage of the Dartford-Thurrock Crossing Bill through Parliament in the 1987/88 Session work started in August 1988 on the construction of a new bridge which with the tunnels and associated improvements to the A282 approach roads will double the capacity of this important Thames crossing. The bridge is on schedule for opening in Summer 1991. Design and construction of the bridge is being privately financed by Dartford River Crossing Ltd who took over responsibility for the operation of the crossing under a concession agreement on 31 July 1988. This is the first example in modern times of a major piece of road infrastructure being provided by the private sector. Further provision of trunk road infrastructure by the private sector is being actively pursued. Proposals were invited in April 1989 for the provision of a second Severn Bridge on the basis of a design, build, finance and operate scheme and a design and build scheme with construction and operation being publicly financed. Proposals from two consortia have been shortlisted and it is hoped to announce a final decision soon. Three consortia have pre-qualified to bid for constructing and financing the Birmingham Northern Relief Road. The Government will be ready to consider proposals for the private finance of other schemes listed in this report where this would offer improved value for money.

Forward programme

3.5   Table 3 gives details of all national trunk road schemes in preparation at 1 January 1990, including the new schemes announced in "Roads For Prosperity". Table 3 also includes twenty additional schemes identified since publication of the White Paper and now included in the programme for the first time. They are:-

Route Number	Scheme
M2	Widening between Junctions 3 & 4
M4	Widening between Junctions 12 & 15
A2	Kidbrooke Park Road Interchange
A2	Lydden (B2060) -- Dover Improvement
A3	M25 -- A245 Improvement
A12	Whalebone Lane Junction Improvement
A12	Gallows Corner Intersection Improvement
A30	Woodleigh Grade Separated Junction
A30	Carland Cross -- Zelah Improvement
A31	Stag Gate Improvement
A31	Winterborne Zelston Improvement
A40	Long Lane -- West End Road
A49	Craven Arms Bypass
A66	Temple Sowerby Bypass and Improvement to Winderwath
A66	Longnewton Grade Separated Junction
A140	Beacon Hill (A45) -- Scole Improvement
A406	Ironbridge -- Neasden Improvement
A435/A438	South of Evesham -- M5 Improvement
A523	Packsaddle -- Rushton Spencer Improvement
A523	Miles Knoll -- Waterhouses Improvement

Also included in Table 3 are six former regional schemes whose estimated cost has exceeded £1 million.

3.6   The total mileage of schemes in the programme at 1 January 1990 was over 2,500 miles. This includes 170 miles of new motorway, widening of almost 600 miles of existing motorway and conversion of 43 miles of all-purpose sections of A1 to motorway. Completion of this programme will result in nearly one third of the motorway network being dual 4-lane standard and most of the remainder being dual 3-lane standard. The length of all-purpose dual carriageway trunk road will be doubled, with nearly two thirds being dual carriageway standard.

3.7   The proposed standard of schemes in the programme prior to the publication of the new 1989 National Road Traffic Forecasts has been reviewed. In certain cases schemes will have to be designed to a higher standard. This, and the further additions that have been made to the programme, brings the total works cost of the programme to £12.4 billion (in November 1987 prices, excluding VAT, the basis used in "Roads For Prosperity" to cost the expanded programme).

3.8   The programme will mean improvements to the trunk road network in all regions of the country. Key schemes are widening to dual four-lane standard a 134 miles of the M1 between the M25 and M18 in Yorkshire, over 80 miles of the M6 between the M1 and Manchester, and over 100 miles of the M25 around London. Major new all-purpose trunk road schemes include further improvements to the A1 between London and Newcastle, dualling the A11 between the M11 and Norwich and improvements to the A30/A303 route to the South West. Further details are given in the regional summaries (see Section 10).

3.9   "Roads For Prosperity" also announced a number of major studies. These include examination of the possibility of upgrading the remaining all-purpose sections of the A1 between London and Tyneside to motorway standard; a Trans-Pennine study (for which consultants have recently been appointed) to examine provision of additional capacity between South Lancashire and Yorkshire; and a Lower Thames Crossing Study.

Delivering the programme

3.10   "Roads For Prosperity" acknowledged that the size and urgency of the new programme would require additional resources and new organisational arrangements. A new Road Programme Director with executive responsibility for the management of the programme has been appointed.

3.11   Project management of trunk road schemes will be undertaken by staff dedicated to this task. This will be achieved by two main changes to the regional organisation of the Department of Transport:

>   - a new Motorway Widening Unit is being set up in Coventry to deal with motorway widening schemes, which represent about one third of the value of the programme;

>   - most of the existing regional offices will be split into dedicated Construction Programme and Network Management Divisions.

The Construction Programme Divisions will be responsible for national programme schemes over £5 million in value. They and the Motorway Widening Unit will report to the Road Programme Director. The Regional Directors will retain their existing responsibilities for advising both the Secretaries of State for the Environment and for Transport on planning and environmental issues and on statutory decisions on trunk road schemes. This will ensure that full weight continues to be given to environmental factors.

3.12 The management and maintenance of the network and the smaller construction schemes will be dealt with by the Network Management Divisions. Thus network management will also be focussed within a more dedicated organisational structure with resultant benefits. The Network Management Divisions will continue to report to the Regional Directors.

3.13 In addition, greater use will be made of the private sector. Firms of consulting engineers with appropriate experience have been invited, on a competitive basis, to provide staff to work on project management and specialist functions alongside civil servants in the new regional organisation.

Action to commission new schemes

3.14 Letting of commissions for the schemes added to the programme by "Roads For Prosperity" began promptly in Summer 1989 and is being phased in order to allow the Department to spread design and supervision opportunities among consultants to its best advantage. So far, a total of 43 commissions have been let with a total schemes value of over £1 billion. Of these, 37 commissions have been awarded to private consultants with the remainder being awarded to agent authorities. In addition, 8 studies with a total value of £5.6 million have been let; 6 to private consultants and 2 to agent authorities. It is intended to keep up steady progress on commission letting with the emphasis on making best use of the considerable engineering expertise available and obtaining good value for money through competitive procedures. The next batch of commissions is likely to be let in early Spring.

Timing of the programme

3.15 The largest element of time taken to complete a trunk road scheme is in the pre-construction stages. These include statutory procedures to authorise a scheme, which ensure that those whose rights or interests are affected by proposals have the chance of a full and fair hearing. It is not proposed to change these statutory procedures.

3.16 It was announced at the beginning of 1988 that steps were being taken to speed up the pre-statutory preparation stages of schemes. Already there are indications that preparation times are being reduced. Establishment of the dedicated Construction Programme Divisions and Motorway Widening Unit will further the objective of speeding up the early preparation of schemes.

3.17 For each scheme in the programme the next key preparation stage and the target date by when it is expected to be reached is shown in Table 3. An expected start of works date is indicated for those schemes where the Highways Act orders have been made. Annex A gives further details of scheme preparation stages.

4   VALUE FOR MONEY

4.1 A modern industrial society demands a transport system able to move goods rapidly and efficiently from the points of production to the consumer. Raw materials must be delivered to the point of manufacture. Some materials and products may be especially suited to rail, but generally road transport is preferred by industry. The availability of good roads is a key consideration in locating new businesses or relocating existing businesses. Reliability of deliveries is important for industry. Increasing car ownership and use for business, domestic and leisure purposes means that the motorist too demands a road system enabling journeys to be made in reasonable times and safety. Thus the trunk road network plays a very significant part in the functioning of the economy and the way we live.

4.2 However major trunk road schemes are very costly and it is important that proposals are scrutinised carefully to ensure that they represent good value for money. Economic benefits are a high priority, but not the only objective of the trunk road programme. As with any ill thought out development a badly located and insensitively designed road scheme can be highly damaging. The environmental impact of proposed schemes is therefore assessed as well. Together the economic and environmental assessments inform the decision making process.

Economic assessment

4.3 The economic return from trunk road schemes is assessed from the earliest stages through to detailed design of the selected route. A scheme is normally required to show a positive net economic benefit if it is to be progressed to construction. The main benefit usually comes from time savings. Estimates are made of the benefits to road users over 30 years of reducing journey times, and changes in vehicle operating costs and the number and severity of accidents. The cost of any delays to road users while works are carried out are also estimated.

4.4 The appraisal techniques used are periodically examined by the independent Standing Advisory Committee on Trunk Road Assessment (SACTRA) to see if they are sound and appropriate for the full range of road schemes. SACTRA has endorsed the current appraisal methods used. COBA and QUADRO are the standard computer programs for estimating the net benefit from motorway and other trunk road schemes although in certain cases alternative techniques are used (see paragraph 4.5). These appraisal programs have been continually improved and updated. COBA estimates the scheme benefits to road users. The QUADRO program estimates the cost of delays to road users caused by construction and maintenance works which affect the existing road. The costs and benefits are discounted at 8 per cent, the same rate as is used in the assessment of other transport investments. The overall trunk road programme is likely to show a benefit to cost ratio of 2.5:1. This is broadly equivalent to a rate of return of 20 per cent.

Urban schemes

4.5 New sophisticated traffic modelling techniques are being applied to appraising congested urban traffic conditions. In urban areas there are severe limits to the amount of road space that can be provided. The capacity of the road network in the neighbourhood of the road improvement sets constraints on possible traffic levels. The forecasting of traffic growth constrained in this way is now an essential element of London trunk road scheme appraisal and the methods developed there may find application in other urban scheme appraisals.

Environmental assessment

4.6 For a decade now, following the Leitch report in 1977, it has been standard practice to undertake an environmental assessment of trunk road schemes. The Department of Transport Manual of Environmental Appraisal was published in 1983. An environmental appraisal has been one of the documents made available as a matter of routine at public inquiries into proposed schemes. The implementation of EEC Directive 85/337 on environmental assessment of major developments in July 1988 required the publication of an environmental statement on all major trunk road schemes and any scheme over 1km passing through or within 100m of a national park, a site of special scientific interest, nature reserve or conservation area.

4.7 Environmental assessments are carried out by means of a framework analysis entailing an estimate of the changes due to the construction and operation of a new or widened road. A number of factors are considered in the analysis including noise, severance, air pollution and effects on wildlife. While it is not the policy, on the advice of SACTRA, to place a monetary value on the environmental impact of schemes the environmental assessment is, as already indicated, considered alongside the economic assessment. Environmental factors can and sometimes do outweigh economic considerations in making a final choice. Schemes which do not show a net economic benefit may be undertaken when environmental benefits are judged to outweigh quantifiable economic disbenefits. An example of a scheme where this has happened is the A69 Brampton Bypass, which is under construction.

4.8 A study is being made of techniques proposed for the monetary evaluation of environmental changes and the values used in other countries in highway decisions. SACTRA is to consider again monetary evaluation of the environmental impact of schemes.

Standards

4.9 The Department of Transport provides technical advice and direction on the design, construction and operation of roads so as to ensure efficiency and consistency throughout the network. The Department issues Standards and Advice Notes on a wide variety of subjects, the objective being to ensure value for money in terms of long term performance and durability and safety. The Single Market in 1992 and the increasing adoption of harmonised standards throughout the European Community will provide further opportunities to achieve value for money, from greater competition and standardisation.

Project management

4.10 The efficient management of projects can also improve value for money. A project manager is appointed for each major trunk road scheme, whose responsibility is to progress the scheme through the statutory procedures, supervise the consultants or agent undertaking the design, ensure an optimum solution which meets all the requirements, and during construction to ensure proper execution of works within the contract price. Expansion of the programme places a large demand upon project management resources and as noted in paragraph 3.13 joint Project Management Teams, drawing on the resources of both the Department of Transport and the private sector, will be created to achieve effective project control.

Purchasing

4.11 It is essential to obtain best value for money for the very considerable sums spent in purchasing the services of consultants and contractors for highway projects. In order to improve procurement practices, a report was commissioned by an independent consultant, Mr Frank Griffiths. In the light of the consideration of the report proposals are at an advanced stage of development; but outside interests will be consulted where appropriate before decisions are taken.

5   IMPROVING THE ENVIRONMENT

5.1 Heavy volumes of traffic passing through a town or village damage the environment for those who live and work there. The risk of accidents is increased; there is the problem of noise; air quality will be reduced by exhaust emissions, particularly if there is congestion; vibrations can be transmitted to buildings and be a source of annoyance to occupants. Removing through traffic provides residents with a safer, cleaner and quieter environment. The provision of bypasses for towns and villages is a continuing feature of the trunk road programme. Since April 1987 thirty-seven bypasses have been completed including ones for Evesham, Saltash and Wetherby. There are over one hundred and fifty bypass and relief road schemes in the present programme.

5.2 While bypasses improve the local environment of towns and villages, like other schemes they have a wider impact. Where proposed schemes are likely to affect designated areas, such as Sites of Special Scientific Interest or Areas of Outstanding Natural Beauty particular care is taken to do as little damage as possible. To this end interested bodies such as the Nature Conservancy Council and local environment groups are consulted. The prime means of minimising the environmental impact of schemes rests in the choice of route and sympathetic design of associated structures. Advice on such matters is provided by the independent Landscape Advisory Committee and the Royal Fine Art Commission. Landscape architects and horticulturalists are involved in the design of schemes. The way in which landscape measures such as contouring and planting can help to blend a road into the surrounding landscape is illustrated in Figure 3. To minimise the impact on wildlife, features such as badger tunnels have been incorporated into schemes.

Figure 3   CONTOURING AND PLANTING TO BLEND ROAD INTO LANDSCAPE

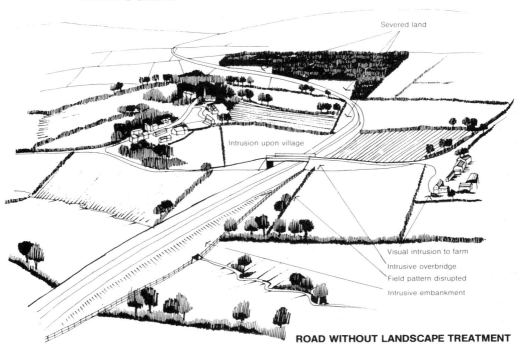

ROAD WITHOUT LANDSCAPE TREATMENT

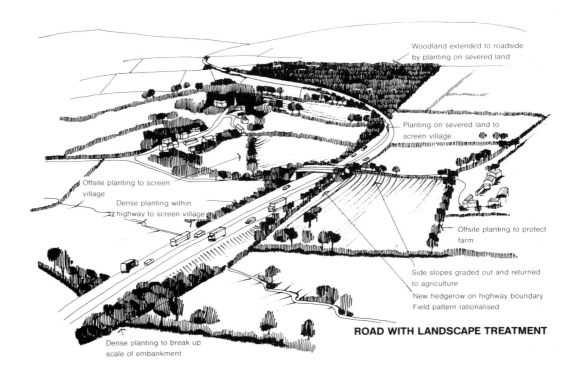

ROAD WITH LANDSCAPE TREATMENT

M40 motorway

5.3   The care taken to mitigate the environmental impact of a scheme is illustrated by the M40 now under construction. Much of the motorway passes through attractive countryside. Several routes including that now under construction were assessed in terms of their effects upon the landscape, agriculture, nature conservation and planning policies and people living nearby. The selected route takes maximum advantage of the contours or cover provided by existing trees. There has been considerable use of earth mounds to create false cuttings in order to preserve views. The cross-sections shown in Figure 4 illustrate two examples from the Warmington Valley, a particularly scenic part of the route north of Banbury. The lines of sight show how the mounds and proposed tree planting combine to screen views of the motorway from Farnborough Obelisk, a notable viewpoint. Cross-section A shows the grading of the slope facing the viewpoint to a shallow angle so that it can be returned to agricultural use making the earthwork indistinguishable from the surrounding fields, even more effectively disguising the presence of the motorway. Cross-section B shows the motorway being screened with a combination of contouring and planting.

5.4   Some 750,000 trees and shrubs will be planted throughout the length of the M40. Planting will not be confined to the roadworks. Some will be on land acquired for the purpose of planting in order to blend the motorway more effectively into the landscape. There are also schemes for "off-site" planting on private land under arrangements agreed with landowners. Off-site planting closer to affected viewpoints can provide quicker and more effective screening and can be carried out in advance of construction. A large programme of off-site planting in connection with the M40 has been under way since 1986. On the section north of Wendlebury 33 schemes have been completed and a further 34 are under negotiation. A similar programme of off-site planting is planned for the southern section between Waterstock and Wendlebury.

5.5   Motorway verges provide an area free from day to day human interference and hence act as a refuge for wildlife. The value of the M40 for wildlife will be further enhanced by the seeding of some 14 hectares of selected verge with a special seed mix of wildflowers and grasses. Species will include Ox-eye Daisy, Cowslip, Knapweed, Lady's Smock and Meadow Cranesbill. The sowing of key areas will assist colonisation of the rest of the motorway with wildflowers.

5.6   One aspect of construction which can have significant implications in landscape terms is the disposal of surplus spoil material. Every effort is made to balance cut and fill at the design stage, but this may not be physically possible. An example is the section of the M40 north of Warwick, where the motorway had to be kept in cutting to shield adjacent villages. In this case arrangements had to be made for off-site disposal of a significant quantity of surplus material. The Department of Transport project management team and landscape architects have been actively involved in discussions with the planning authorities and contractors and advising on the environmental aspects of spoil disposal. As a result several off-site disposal sites alongside the M40 have been sensitively shaped and successfully integrated with the surrounding landscape.

Figure 4

M40 MOTORWAY CONTOURING AND PLANTING

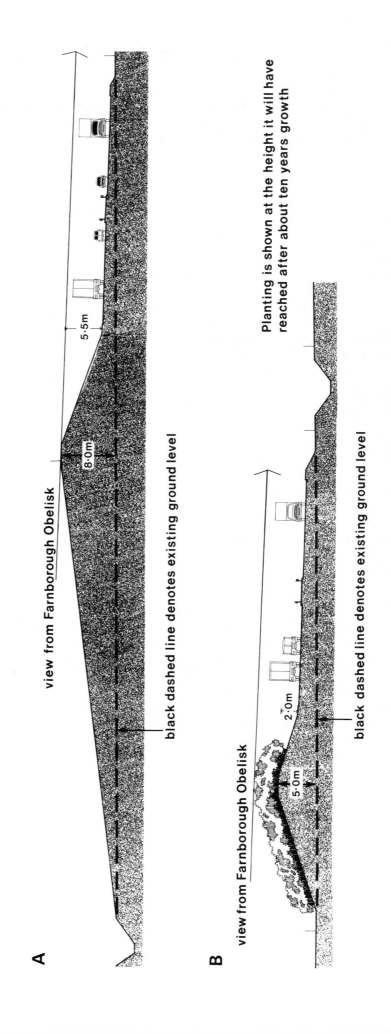

A

view from Farnborough Obelisk

5·5m

8·0m

black dashed line denotes existing ground level

B

view from Farnborough Obelisk

Planting is shown at the height it will have reached after about ten years growth

5·0m

2·0m

black dashed line denotes existing ground level

Enhancement of environmental treatment of schemes

5.7   While the example of the M40 demonstrates the care already taken over the environmental treatment of trunk road schemes a review has been undertaken of what further measures might help to minimise damage to the environment and heritage while meeting the demands for road transport. As a result new initiatives are to be taken on landscape treatment and the environmental aspects of scheme design, the funding of archaeological investigations in advance of works, and dealing with the problem of noise.

5.8   Consultants are to be appointed to advise the Department of Transport on the best landscape and environmental practice on schemes for motorway widening and new trunk roads. A best practice note on environmental scheme design is to be prepared. Consultants are to be appointed to follow up a study that has already been undertaken on environmental treatment of urban schemes. Their task will be to advise on how to put the findings of the study into practice and produce a guidance note on environmental treatment of urban schemes. More resources will be devoted to landscape works and planting. Staffing in this area will be increased by 50 per cent including dedicated teams for the new Motorway Widening Unit and the Construction Programme Divisions in the Eastern, North West, South East and West Midland Regions. The Department of Transport already plants some two million trees each year. This number will substantially increase as the programme set out in this report is carried forward. As well as new schemes it is proposed to improve the landscape and appearance of existing roads, especially in urban areas.

5.9   The Department of Transport already makes an annual payment of £100,000 to English Heritage to fund archaeological survey and excavation work in advance of schemes. It is proposed to increase the annual payment to £500,000.

5.10   There will be greater exercise of discretionary powers relating to the provision of noise insulation. Houses near to motorways or other roads which are being widened will be treated on a basis similar to that which applies to the construction of new roads.

5.11   The new initiatives outlined above will augment existing initiatives on provision of less intrusive lighting and recycling of materials for road construction.

Consultation

5.12   Early consultation and constructive dialogue are important in identifying the scope for resolving conflicts between the need for road improvements and the desire to preserve the environment. The Government remains committed to consulting environmental organisations as early as possible on individual schemes.

6   IMPROVING SAFETY

6.1   While Britain has one of the best road safety records in western Europe deaths and injuries from road accidents continue at a high level. There were over 300,000 road accident casualties in Britain in 1988 with some 63,000 people seriously injured and 5,000 killed. This is an unacceptable toll. The Government set a target in 1987 of reducing road casualties by one third by the end of the century.

6.2   The majority of accidents happen on local roads in built up areas, but many occur on motorways and other trunk roads. There were over 5,500 motorway accident casualties in Britain in 1988 with 845 people seriously injured and 215 killed. New and improved roads are safer than the ones they replace. Safety is a major consideration in the design of schemes. The scope for accident reduction is one of the factors taken into account in selecting schemes for the national trunk road programme. Overall accident savings account for some 18 per cent of the total benefits from trunk road improvement schemes.

6.3   New criteria for the installation of central reserve safety fences on all-purpose dual carriageway trunk roads were announced in 1986. The policy is to install such fencing on all new dual carriageway schemes; on existing dual carriageways where major maintenance is being carried out and in other cases where justified by traffic levels. In the financial years 1987/88 and 1988/89 some 440 miles of new central reserve fencing were installed on all-purpose dual carriageway trunk roads and a further 280 miles will have been installed in 1989/90.

6.4   Improper use by drivers of emergency crossing points in the central reserve of motorways has resulted in some serious accidents in the past few years. The policy is to close these crossing points except where their retention has been deemed essential by the emergency services for operational reasons. At the begining of 1989 there were just over 1,000 emergency crossing points. Closure of 70 per cent of these has been programmed for completion by the end of March 1990.

6.5   Since the beginning of 1988 the skidding resistance of the trunk road network has been monitored on a routine basis using the sideways force coefficient routine investigation machine - SCRIM - developed by the Transport and Road Research Laboratory. It is estimated that the resultant treatment to bring roads up to the new standards of skidding resistance will save 1800 casualties a year. The intention is to survey the entire network on a three-year cycle.

6.6   In some places a low cost engineering scheme may help to eliminate an accident problem. Local highway authorities have been encouraged to undertake such schemes on their roads. Steps were taken in 1989 to enhance the effort on trunk road local safety schemes. Target numbers for such local safety schemes and guideline budgets have been set for each Department of Transport region.

6.7   Accidents usually lead to delays for other road users. On a heavily used motorway or trunk roads long traffic queues can build up very quickly following an accident. Reacting speedily to accidents is thus very important and ways of improving the response to accidents and incidents are being evaluated. On two heavily used sections of motorway - 50 miles of the M1 in Bedfordshire, Buckinghamshire and Northamptonshire and the M4 westbound approach to the Severn Bridge in Avon - traffic surveillance systems have been installed which detect queues or slow moving vehicles automatically and, in a matter of seconds, warn the Police and activate the warning signals. The intention is for these systems to be used increasingly on the motorway network.

6.8   Another safety related development is the installation of fog detectors around the M25. The fog detectors will automatically display the legend FOG on the warning signals as visibility falls below a pre-set level, giving a warning to drivers before they reach the section of motorway where fog has formed. The signals will be switched off automatically as the fog clears.

6.9   The Department of Transport has also been working with its agents and the police to reduce the time for which carriageways are obstructed and improve advance warning and information to other drivers. To this end a trial has been undertaken with Kent County Council. This involved improvements to the council's county-wide VHF radio communications system and the issue of radio pagers to all key staff. Closer liaison was also established with the police. The results of the trial are now being analysed to identify those cost effective elements which could be introduced nationally.

6.10   The Department of Transport has a continuing programme of research into methods of improving road safety. The results are applied to existing as well as to new roads. Recent safety research has resulted in improvements to traffic signs and signals; better road layout and junction design; skid resistant surfaces; more widespread use of safety fencing; and better road markings. In addition, the Department will shortly be introducing road safety audits of all new road schemes.

7 ASSISTING REGENERATION OF INNER CITIES

7.1 The Government is committed to the regeneration of inner city areas so that they too have a chance to share in the nation's prosperity. Many suffer from transport problems. Provision of good transport links is vital if inner cities are to reach their full potential.

7.2 Since the trunk road network is designed to cater for the needs of through traffic, there are few trunk roads actually in urban areas. The construction and improvement of trunk roads can nevertheless help to restore the vitality of inner city areas by relieving traffic congestion making them more attractive places for people to live and work. Good road links to other parts of the country encourage location of businesses in the inner areas by improving reliability and speed of distribution. Thus inner city areas stand to benefit from the expansion of the trunk road programme. It is estimated that some £2.5 billion of motorway and trunk road schemes planned or under construction will directly benefit inner cities. Examples are:

- M66 Denton-Middleton (Manchester Outer Ring Road)

- Western Orbital Route, West Midlands

- A1/M1 Link south east of Leeds

- A1 Newcastle Western Bypass

There has been good progress on the two new schemes announced as part of the Action For Cities initiative launched in 1988. Construction work will start soon on the A13 improvements in London's Docklands and, subject to completion of statutory procedures, construction work should start on the Black Country Spine Road in the West Midlands this Summer.

7.3 The local road network in inner city areas is the responsibility of the local highway authorities. Improvements to local highways which are of more than local importance can be supported by Transport Supplementary Grant (TSG). Benefits to inner city areas are now an important factor in the selection of schemes to be financed with the help of TSG, and the 1989 circular from the Department of Transport to local highway authorities inviting bids for TSG in 1990/91 drew special attention to urban regeneration. During 1990/91 TSG will support expenditure of over £160 million on major schemes which will directly benefit inner city areas, an increase of almost 50 per cent on 1987/88. Over 100 major inner city highway improvements, costing £1 billion, will then be supported by TSG including:

- Birmingham Heartlands Spine Road (£85m)

- Bradford City Ring Road (£37m)

- St Helens Link Road (£31m)

- Middlesbrough Bypass (£26m)

- Lewisham Town Centre Improvement (£30m)

7.4 Grant under the Industrial Development Act is also available to developers and local authorities for schemes in Assisted Areas, which will create new jobs in inner city areas. The Department of Transport is paying grant of up to £4 million towards access to the Meadowhall development in Sheffield. In Rotherham grant of nearly £2 million is being paid towards improvement of access to developments which it is expected will create some 2,000 new jobs in an area of high unemployment.

8 MAINTENANCE AND MANAGEMENT OF THE TRUNK ROAD NETWORK

8.1 The trunk road network requires regular maintenance to keep it in safe condition and good state of repair. Maintenance ranges from routine tasks such as sweeping and grass cutting to major structural work including complete reconstruction. The day to day work involved in maintaining the network is a task carried out by local agents (county councils, metropolitan district councils, London boroughs) and, in some cases by consulting engineers acting as agents, under the overall management of the regional offices of the Department of Transport.

8.2 The objectives of the capital maintenance programme are to preserve past investment in the road system at minimum cost and with minimum disruption to road traffic, and to ensure that roads are safe and offer a reasonably comfortable quality of ride. In addition the opportunity may be taken to increase the strength of the road to deal with increasing traffic.

8.3 The condition of flexible carriageways on the trunk road network is kept under constant review through the combined use of routine machine and visual surveys. Machine surveys using the Deflectograph record the deflection of a pavement under a heavy wheel load. By analysing the deflection together with pavement construction and traffic loading an estimate can be made of the remaining life of the road. The data can also be used to design strengthening overlays when the remaining life becomes very short. Visual surveys are done under the Computerised Highway Assessment of Ratings and Treatments (CHART) system. Visible defects such as rutting, cracking and surface deterioration are recorded and the data processed by computer programs which calculate ratings of defectiveness. The ratings are used to identify lengths of sub-standard road and the treatment required with a priority for action. A system of visual assessment for concrete roads was introduced in 1988, recognising the characteristics of deterioration unique to this type of road.

8.4 During 1990 the High Speed Road Monitor will be brought into routine use. This machine, which scans road surfaces using lasers to identify defects while travelling at 50 miles per hour, can identify early signs of structural deterioration without the need for lane closures and hence reduce traffic disruption. It will allow detailed inspections to be targeted on the sections of road most in need of attention.

8.5 Having detailed knowledge of the condition of the network from routine surveys enables effective planning of maintenance and the best use of available resources. The aim is to carry out major renewal at the optimum time: it is especially important to overlay a road before deterioration reaches the point at which reconstruction, costing three times as much, becomes necessary.

8.6 The Department of Transport and local highway authorities are jointly developing a new management system for structural maintenance of roads. This will enable the very large amounts of data on road condition provided by high-speed machine surveys to be stored and analysed to identify maintenance need and develop cost effective programmes of treatment.

Minimising delays at maintenance works

8.7 Maintenance work can cause delay and inconvenience to road users. Efforts are made to minimise such delays, but in some cases they are unavoidable. Major maintenance works are programmed wherever possible when traffic is lightest. On dual carriageways two-way flows on the same carriageway whenever practical are designed not to exceed two miles in length and with spaces of at least six miles between sites. Night time working is employed where possible especially for survey and routine work, and seasonal traffic peaks are avoided. Mobile lane closures will be increasingly employed for maintenance work such as line-painting, carried out under the cover and protection of a convoy of moving vehicles with mounted signs to give clear indications to motorists of the works ahead.

8.8 Provision of advance information about major works through regular bulletins and publicity leaflets, the motoring organisations and the media assists drivers to plan journeys to avoid likely trouble spots. The Department is looking at ways to improve the quality, reliability and prompt dissemination of information on road conditions to drivers by the use of new technology and closer links with the media. Improved signs and signals on motorways are also planned to provide more information about roadworks and traffic conditions ahead.

8.9 The more quickly maintenance works are carried out, the shorter the period of inconvenience to road users. The system of lane rental contracts has been used on many major maintenance schemes since 1984 with the objective of speeding up works. A contractor receives a bonus if works are completed ahead of schedule, but incurs a lane rental charge if there is an overrun. To date this system has saved over 2,000 days of delays. As contractors accustomed to lane rental contracts have developed new methods and technology for completing works in the shortest time, conventional contracts are also being completed more quickly. The use of lane rental contracts is expected to continue on a selective basis which avoids pushing up costs .

8.10 Other ways of increasing capacity at roadworks are being considered. In some circumstances tidal flow systems can be used where there is two-way working to reverse the flow in a particular lane to deal with peak traffic flows. If it can be done safely narrower lanes are used past roadworks to facilitate the continued free flow of traffic.

8.11 New design standards for trunk roads were introduced in 1987. Roads are now designed to have a life of forty years for estimated traffic flows before major reconstruction is necessary. For flexible construction "blacktop" roads, strengthening by overlay will normally be required after twenty years in order to renew the road for the remainder of its design life. In the longer term these new standards should mean the overall need for maintenance and associated delays to traffic will be reduced.

Structural maintenance

8.12 Existing motorways have generally lasted well and carried far greater volumes of traffic than originally expected. Major reconstruction has been required on average after about twenty years, so that about 5 per cent of the network has needed to be renewed every year in order to keep pace with deterioration.

8.13 Structural maintenance consists mainly of reconstruction, overlaying and resurfacing and major repairs to earthworks. The aim is to identify a forward programme of major renewal schemes to provide greater commitment in the forward planning and programming of schemes. The level of major maintenance activity has varied over the years. In the mid-70s the emphasis was on new construction rather than maintenance and, together with a real cutback in maintenance expenditure in 1977/78 and unexpectedly high traffic growth, this resulted in a substantial backlog of major maintenance work. At the end of 1989/90 these estimated backlogs of renewal are expected to be 48 equivalent route miles of motorway and 189 single carriageway equivalent miles of other trunk road, and an average annual renewal of 86 miles of motorway and 236 miles of other trunk road is required for the next three years to keep pace with deterioration and eliminate the remaining backlog. The results of deflection surveys are being analysed to review the requirements for renewal.

Routine maintenance and litter collection

8.14 Routine maintenance comprises short term cyclic work such as patching, street cleaning, shrub trimming and grass cutting required to keep a road in a safe condition. The aim is to ensure that routine tasks are carried out uniformly by agents and in the most cost effective manner. A code of practice on routine maintenance introduced in 1985 places work on a needs led basis taking account of local conditions and avoiding costly over provision.

Together with the computerised Routine Maintenance Management Information System the code is helping to achieve consistency, better value for money, better allocation of resources and a longer term reduction in the amount of structural maintenance.

8.15 It is proposed under the Environmental Protection Bill before Parliament to clarify responsibility for street cleaning. Instead of the present arrangements which involve both highway authorities and district councils in the collection of litter, all litter collection will be the responsibility of local district and borough councils. However litter collection on trunk motorways, where special considerations of traffic movement and safety apply, will remain the responsibility of the Department of Transport.

Bridge maintenance

8.16 An expanded capital maintenance programme for trunk road bridges planned over 15 years and costing £1 billion, was begun in 1988. It consists of three elements:

- assessment and strengthening where necessary of bridges and other structures to meet the demands of modern heavy lorries, including the introduction of lorries with a maximum gross weight of 40 tonnes in 1999, when the present EC derogation (which allows the UK to limit gross weight to 38 tonnes) expires;

- ''steady state'' maintenance such as concrete repairs and repainting, to deal with wear and tear and deterioration;

- upgrading or strengthening certain features such as piers and columns and waterproofing bridge decks.

8.17 The strength of about 2,200 older bridges in England will be assessed; over half of these assessments are either under way or complete. The remaining assessments are scheduled to be completed by 1991. The cost of the overall programme is reviewed and updated as assessments progressively yield information on different aspects of bridge condition. Estimates will also take account of the results of research under way on the strength of reinforced concrete bridges built between 1961 and 1973 and the loading standards for long span bridges. The research is expected to lead to the need for further assessment and strengthening of these types of bridges.

Local bridges

8.18 Local highway authorities also have much work to do to improve and strengthen bridges on their own roads. The Government provided for £27million extra expenditure on bridge assessment and strengthening in England as part of the Rate Support Grant Settlement for 1989/90, and a similar amount has been allowed for in the Revenue Support Grant settlement for 1990/91. However, it was announced in November 1989 that the Government proposed to re-classify all structural maintenance on roads as capital instead of current expenditure, in a phased programme starting in 1991/92. The expenditure would become eligible for Transport Supplementary Grant as it was transferred across, and the first tranche would be for bridge assessment and strengthening. Department of Transport regional offices will be liaising with local authorities to help ensure that work on trunk and other roads is properly coordinated to ensure that any delays and diversions as a result of bridge work are kept to a minimum.

Winter maintenance

8.19 Important elements of good winter maintenance are the precautionary salting of roads and prompt clearing of snow. Modern ice detection systems are operated by many agents in conjunction with weather forecasts to provide local forecasts of road temperature conditions. These systems enable better and timely decisions to be made, reducing the amount of salt used and providing a more cost effective service. Winter maintenance of the motorways involves a fleet of 295 specialist salting and ploughing vehicles based at 94 maintenance compounds located at strategic points of the network. A proportion of these vehicles are maintained in a reserve which can be deployed in times of exceptionally severe conditions and to cover for vehicle breakdowns. Vehicles for the winter maintenance of other trunk roads are provided by agents.

8.20 The Department of Transport has begun to add new salt spreading/snow plough vehicles to its fleet. The existing fleet of vehicles will progressively be replaced by the new generation of vehicles, which are more economical.

Management information systems

8.21 Good management is about predicting the occurrence of problems and taking timely action to deal with them. In a complex enviroment such as that encountered within the highway, sophisticated systems are needed to achieve this objective. A number of independent systems have been in use to deal with specific management issues, but there is now a need to bring these together with newly identified requirements into a single management information system.

8.22 Information technology has an increasing part to play in developing solutions to the problems encountered in highway management and the Department of Transport is committed to its use. Accordingly development of computerised management systems which allow quick and easy access to relevant information and thereby efficient and effective reaction to problems, is regarded as being of high priority. The Network Information System (NIS) currently under development brings together information on traffic, accidents, road condition, works data, project planning and maintenance and construction costs related to a common view of the road network. This system not only assists in decision taking but also enhances this by allowing questions, which could not easily be dealt with previously because of the difficulty of assembling all of the necessary information, to be answered.

9 THE M25 MOTORWAY

9.1 The M25 is the most heavily used road in the country. It is serving much more traffic than was forecast when the road was planned, and is suffering serious congestion at peak hours. Nevertheless the motorway has brought relief to nearby towns and villages and succeded in the objective of taking through traffic out of London. Action has already been taken to deal with the worst congestion problems. The section of the motorway between Junctions 11 and 13 has been widened to dual 4-lane standard. Construction of the new bridge to relieve the Dartford Tunnel is making good progress. The programme announced in "Roads For Prosperity" included a proposal for the remaining 3-lane sections of the M25 to be widened to dual 4-lane standard.

9.2 Consulting engineers Rendel, Palmer and Tritton were commissioned in April 1988 to examine the congestion problems on the M25 and to consider the options for dealing with them. The consultants' report was published in July 1989 (Reference 3). It contained a range of recommendations which have been given careful study having regard to their traffic and environmental implications and the views of a large number of consultees. Plans for further action on the M25 in the light of the consultants' report will be announced soon.

10
REGIONAL REPORTS

NORTHERN

10.1 In the Northern Region the main developments in road infrastructure have been concentrated on the provision of the North-South bypass on the western side of Newcastle upon Tyne together with other improvements of the overall trunk road network. Major schemes costing £190 million are either under construction or in preparation. A study is proposed to consider the longer term requirements of the A1(M).

10.2 Good progress has been made in the £88 million A1 Newcastle Western Bypass. On completion it will link with the existing Gateshead Western Bypass and A1(M) to the south and the A1 to the north to provide a new trunk road on the western side of the Tyne Wear conurbation and remove north/south traffic from Newcastle upon Tyne and Gateshead, improve east/west links and enhance the environment in urban areas. The £13 million A696 Woolsington Bypass connects to the Newcastle Western Bypass and will provide speedier and better access to Newcastle International Airport.

10.3 On the A1 north of Newcastle upon Tyne dual carriageway has been provided as far as Morpeth. Beyond Morpeth it is intended to provide a high standard single carriageway to Scotland with lengths of dual carriageway to allow safer overtaking and improve safety. This is planned at Marshall Meadows, north of Berwick upon Tweed and Brownieside north of Alnwick.

10.4 The A69 has dual carriageway from Newcastle upon Tyne to Hexham. West of Hexham a major improvement is proposed at Haltwhistle and widening schemes and climbing lanes elsewhere will allow safer overtaking.

10.5 Following public consultation the A167 Durham Western Bypass preferred route has been announced. Preparation has commenced on the three new schemes announced in "Roads For Prosperity" to widen the A69 at Gateshead, the A19 in Cleveland and the A167 in Durham.

10.6 Many of the schemes in the Northern Region programme will assist urban regeneration. The Region is involved with Teesside Urban Development Corporation in a Section 278 Agreement scheme in Cleveland, to provide a grade separated junction on the A66. This will enable the redevelopment of the former Stockton Racecourse, and the Teesdale derelict industrial area for business, commerce and leisure. An 85% grant under Section 272 of the Highways Act 1980 is being provided for the Callerton Lane Link Road in Northumberland because of the considerable benefits that the scheme will provide for traffic using the A696 trunk road.

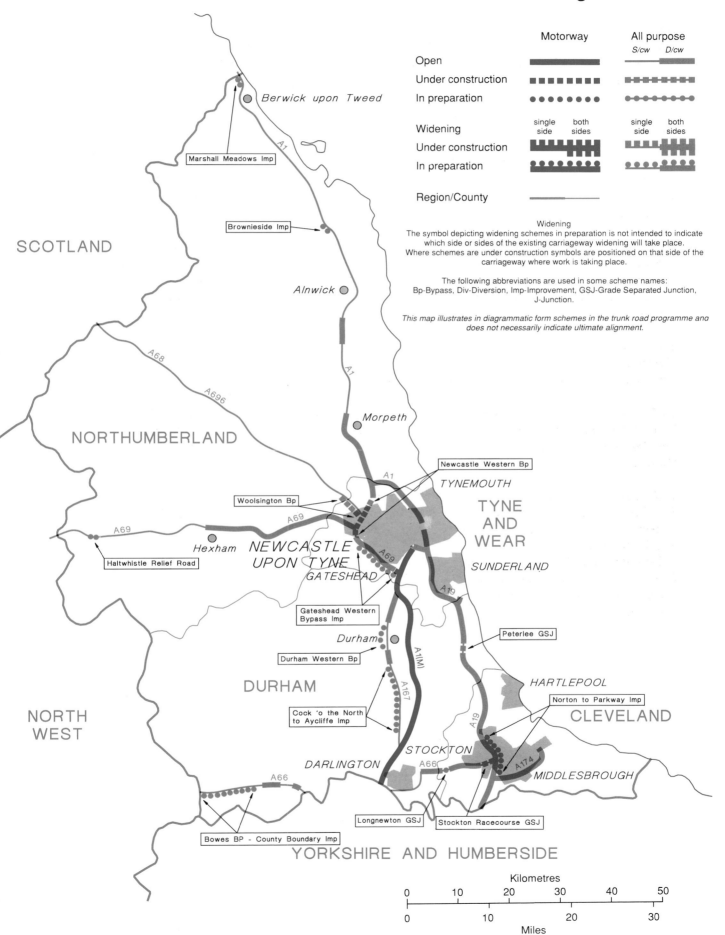

NORTHERN
Schemes costing over £1m

SCOTLAND

Marshall Meadows Imp

● Berwick upon Tweed

Brownieside Imp

Alnwick ●

NORTHUMBERLAND

Morpeth ●

Newcastle Western Bp

Woolsington Bp

TYNEMOUTH

TYNE AND WEAR

A69

Hexham ●

Haltwhistle Relief Road

NEWCASTLE UPON TYNE
GATESHEAD

SUNDERLAND

Gateshead Western Bypass Imp

Durham ●

Durham Western Bp

Peterlee GSJ

HARTLEPOOL

DURHAM

A1(M)

A167

NORTH WEST

Cook 'o the North to Aycliffe Imp

Norton to Parkway Imp

CLEVELAND

A19

STOCKTON

DARLINGTON

A66

MIDDLESBROUGH

A174

Bowes BP - County Boundary Imp

Longnewton GSJ

Stockton Racecourse GSJ

YORKSHIRE AND HUMBERSIDE

Legend

	Motorway	All purpose
		S/cw D/cw
Open		
Under construction		
In preparation		
Widening	single side — both sides	single side — both sides
Under construction		
In preparation		
Region/County		

Widening
The symbol depicting widening schemes in preparation is not intended to indicate which side or sides of the existing carriageway widening will take place. Where schemes are under construction symbols are positioned on that side of the carriageway where work is taking place.

The following abbreviations are used in some scheme names:
Bp-Bypass, Div-Diversion, Imp-Improvement, GSJ-Grade Separated Junction, J-Junction.

This map illustrates in diagrammatic form schemes in the trunk road programme and does not necessarily indicate ultimate alignment.

Kilometres
0   10   20   30   40   50

Miles
0   10   20   30

NORTH WEST

10.7 The North West Region £1.7 billion forward programme is divided roughly equally between new motorway construction, widenings of congested sections of motorway and all-purpose bypasses and improvements.

10.8 Planned new motorway construction is concentrated in and around Greater Manchester with the exception of the northward extension of the M6 in Cumbria. Together with proposals by the Scottish Office the latter will complete a motorway link to Glasgow.

10.9 Priority continues to be given to the completion of the last 10 miles of the Manchester Outer Ring Road - the M66 between Denton and Middleton - and of the associated A6(M) Stockport North South Bypass. The first phase of the upgrading of the Outer Ring Road by widening the two lane section across and near Barton Bridge, is almost complete.

10.10 Other existing sections of the Ring Road are congested with exceptionally high numbers of heavy vehicles, particularly the M62 section north of Manchester. The planned new £300 million motorway, the Greater Manchester Western and Northern Relief Road linking M6 with M66, with crossings of M56, M62 and the Manchester Ship Canal. will relieve several routes in Cheshire and Greater Manchester including that section of M62.

10.11 Widenings costing over £300 million of the M6 through Cheshire, across Thelwall Viaduct, and east of Preston dominate the Region's programme of widenings of congested motorways. The other motorways to be dealt with are the western end of the M62, in Knowsley, and the section east of the planned Greater Manchester Western and Northern Relief Road, and lengths of the M56 and M63 serving Manchester Airport. The Airport will also benefit from one of the Region's planned new all-purpose trunk roads. A dual carriageway is proposed to link the A6(M) Stockport Bypass with M56 near the Airport.

10.12 The largest all-purpose bypass planned is the Preston Southern and Western Bypass, which will include a new crossing of the River Ribble and will link to bypasses proposed towards and around Ormskirk. Other communities which will benefit from bypasses Include Carlisle, Dalton, Disley/High Lane, Poynton, Nantwich, Mottram/Hollingworth/ Tintwistle, Widnes and Wigan/Hindley/Westhoughton.

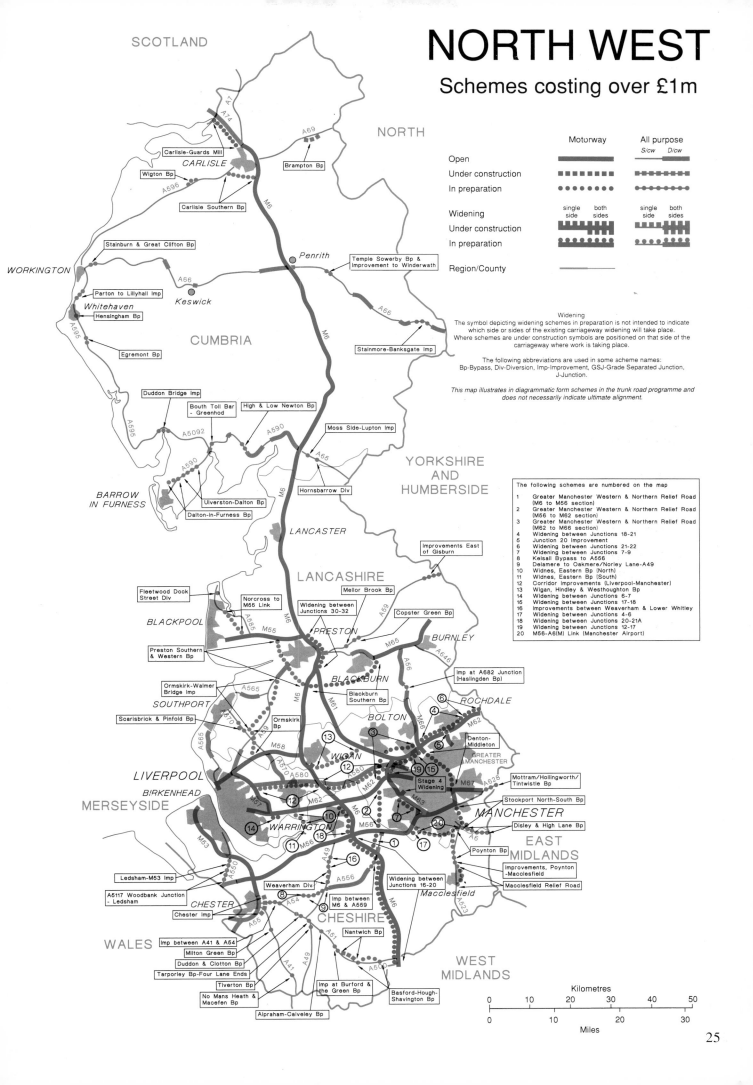

NORTH WEST
Schemes costing over £1m

SCOTLAND

NORTH

Carlisle-Guards Mill
CARLISLE
Wigton Bp
Brampton Bp
Carlisle Southern Bp
A74
A69
A596
M6

Stainburn & Great Clifton Bp
WORKINGTON
Penrith
A66
Temple Sowerby Bp & Improvement to Winderwath
Parton to Lillyhall Imp
Whitehaven
Keswick
Hensingham Bp
CUMBRIA
A66
M6
Stainmore-Banksgate Imp
A595
Egremont Bp

Duddon Bridge Imp
Bouth Toll Bar - Greenhod
High & Low Newton Bp
Moss Side-Lupton Imp
A5092
A590
A65
A590
YORKSHIRE AND HUMBERSIDE
BARROW IN FURNESS
Hornsbarrow Div
A595
M6
Ulverston-Dalton Bp
Dalton-in-Furness Bp
LANCASTER

Improvements East of Gisburn
LANCASHIRE

Fleetwood Dock Street Div
Norcross to M65 Link
Mellor Brook Bp
Widening between Junctions 30-32
Copster Green Bp
BLACKPOOL
M55
M6
PRESTON
A59
BURNLEY
A646
Preston Southern & Western Bp
Imp at A682 Junction (Haslingden Bp)
M65
A565
Ormskirk-Walmer Bridge Imp
A59
BLACKBURN
⑥ ROCHDALE
SOUTHPORT
Blackburn Southern Bp
④
M66
M62
Scarisbrick & Pinfold Bp
A570
Ormskirk Bp
BOLTON
Denton-Middleton
⑬
③
⑤
GREATER MANCHESTER
M58
WIGAN
A580
⑫
M60
⑲ ⑮
Mottram/Hollingworth/Tintwistle Bp
LIVERPOOL
A580
M62
Stage 4 Widening
M67
A628
BIRKENHEAD
M57
⑫
M62
Stockport North-South Bp
MERSEYSIDE
⑭
WARRINGTON
⑩
M6
M56
⑳
MANCHESTER
M53
⑪
M56
⑱
⑦
Disley & High Lane Bp
⑯
A49
①
⑰
A6
EAST MIDLANDS
Ledsham-M53 Imp
Poynton Bp
A6117 Woodbank Junction - Ledsham
Weaverham Div
A556
Widening between Junctions 16-20
Improvements, Poynton -Macclesfield
⑧
Macclesfield
A560
CHESTER
A54
⑨
Imp between M6 & A559
Macclesfield Relief Road
Chester Imp
A55
CHESHIRE
A523
WALES
Imp between A41 & A54
Nantwich Bp
A51
Milton Green Bp
WEST MIDLANDS
Duddon & Clotton Bp
A41
Tarporley Bp-Four Lane Ends
A49
Tiverton Bp
Imp at Burford & the Green Bp
Basford-Hough-Shavington Bp
No Mans Heath & Macefen Bp
A500
Alpraham-Calveley Bp

Legend

	Motorway	All purpose
		S/cw D/cw
Open		
Under construction		
In preparation		
Widening	single side / both sides	single side / both sides
Under construction		
In preparation		
Region/County		

Widening
The symbol depicting widening schemes in preparation is not intended to indicate which side or sides of the existing carriageway widening will take place. Where schemes are under construction symbols are positioned on that side of the carriageway where work is taking place.

The following abbreviations are used in some scheme names:
Bp-Bypass, Div-Diversion, Imp-Improvement, GSJ-Grade Separated Junction, J-Junction.

This map illustrates in diagrammatic form schemes in the trunk road programme and does not necessarily indicate ultimate alignment.

The following schemes are numbered on the map
1 Greater Manchester Western & Northern Relief Road (M6 to M56 section)
2 Greater Manchester Western & Northern Relief Road (M56 to M62 section)
3 Greater Manchester Western & Northern Relief Road (M62 to M66 section)
4 Widening between Junctions 18-21
5 Junction 20 Improvement
6 Widening between Junctions 21-22
7 Widening between Junctions 7-9
8 Kelsall Bypass to A556
9 Delamere to Oakmere/Norley Lane-A49
10 Widnes, Eastern Bp (North)
11 Widnes, Eastern Bp (South)
12 Corridor Improvements (Liverpool-Manchester)
13 Wigan, Hindley & Westhoughton Bp
14 Widening between Junctions 6-7
15 Widening between Junctions 17-18
16 Improvements between Weaverham & Lower Whitley
17 Widening between Junctions 4-6
18 Widening between Junctions 20-21A
19 Widening between Junctions 12-17
20 M56-A6(M) Link (Manchester Airport)

Kilometres
0 10 20 30 40 50

Miles
0 10 20 30

YORKSHIRE AND HUMBERSIDE

10.13 The Yorkshire and Humberside Region forward programme of just under £1 billion concentrates on the improvement of major strategic routes and the provision of environmentally beneficial bypasses on the all-purpose trunk road network.

10.14 One of the most important strategic routes in the region is the A1. Since April 1987 much progress has been made on proposals to upgrade the route throughout the Region. Considerable work has been done in improving junctions. The new interchange recently opened at Dishforth removed the last roundabout from the A1 in Yorkshire. Construction will start in 1990 on the upgrading of the section between Bramham and Wetherby. Other schemes in preparation include the upgrading of the A1 between Doncaster and Hook Moor to motorway standard and widening of the route between Wetherby and Scotch Corner. The possibility of full motorway status for the A1 throughout Yorkshire is being studied.

10.15 In November 1987 plans were announced to construct a new link road between the M1 motorway south of Leeds and the A1. Investigations into the possible route of the scheme have made good progress and public consultation for a motorway route commenced in November 1989. A major trunk road link between the M1 and M62 motorways near Huddersfield will relieve many small communities of the adverse effects of through traffic.

10.16 Other recently announced proposals to improve the Region's motorway network include the widening to dual 4-lane standard of the M1 motorway south of Sheffield and the Pennine section of the M62 motorway west of Huddersfield. Away from the motorway network recent completions include the provision of a high standard all-purpose dual carriageway trunk road between Kildwick and Bingley on the A629/A650 and the A64 Seamer and Crossgates bypass. In addition many smaller communities throughout the Region will benefit environmentally from the provision of local bypasses, including several on the A64, A65 and A19.

YORKSHIRE AND HUMBERSIDE

Schemes costing over £1m

Motorway

Open	
Under construction	
In preparation	single side / both sides

All purpose
S/cw   D/cw

Open	
Under construction	single side
In preparation	both sides

Widening

Under construction	
In preparation	

Region/County

Widening

The symbol depicting widening schemes in preparation is not intended to indicate which side or sides of the existing carriageway widening will take place. Where schemes are under construction symbols are positioned on that side of the carriageway where work is taking place.

The following abbreviations are used in some scheme names:
Bp-Bypass, Div-Diversion, Imp-Improvement, GSJ-Grade Separated Junction, J-Junction.

This map illustrates in diagrammatic form schemes in the trunk road programme and does not necessarily indicate ultimate alignment.

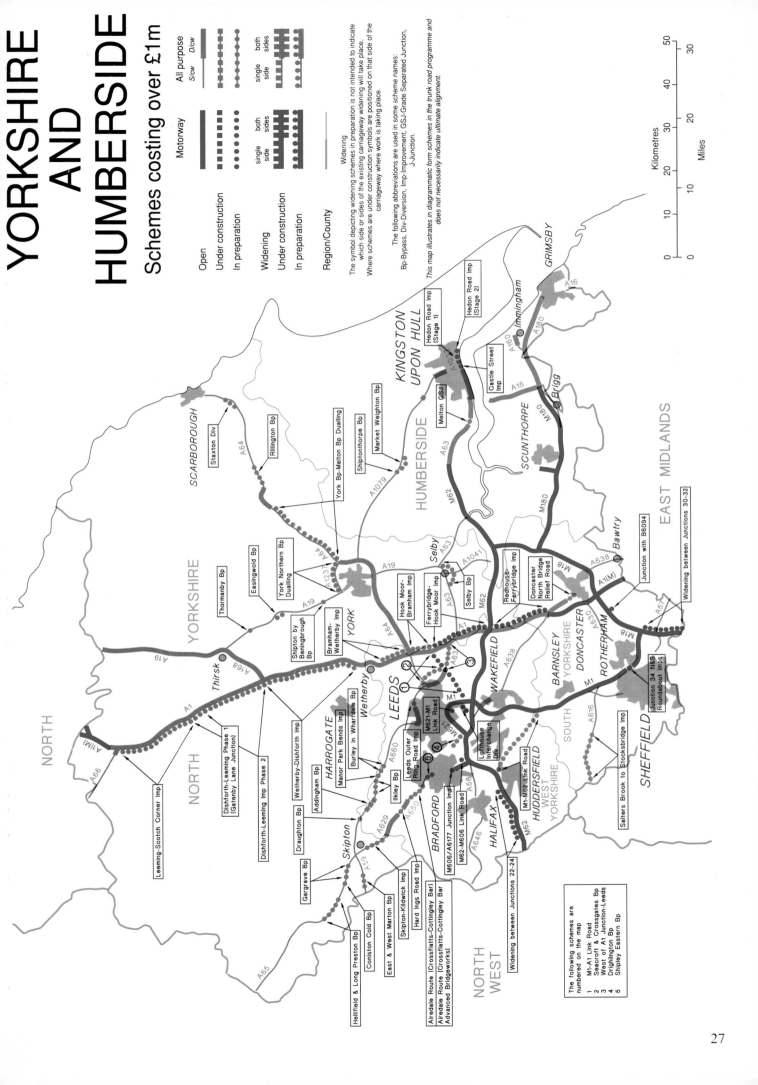

The following schemes are numbered on the map

1 M1-A1 Link Road
2 Seacroft & Crossgates Bp
3 West of A1 Junction-Leeds
4 Drighlington Bp
5 Shipley Eastern Bp

27

WEST MIDLANDS

10.17 The M42 and M54 have been completed and the length of M5 between its M42 junction and Warndon near Worcester has been widened to dual 3-lane carriageway. In addition major new bypasses of Stratford, Coventry, Oswestry, Evesham, Leominster and Newport have been built to improve both driving conditions for trunk road traffic and general conditions within the towns.

10.18 Perhaps most significant for the future economic well-being of the Region has been the progress towards the completion of the M40 with the recent opening of the Warwick Section to traffic and the remaining 6 contracts to complete the extension between Waterstock and the M42 all under way and planned for completion over the next 12 months.

10.19 Other work in progress includes the further widening of M5 between the M42 and Lydiate Ash with its associated M42/M5 Northern Turn and Alcester Bypass. By the middle of 1990 work will have started on the A5/A49 Telford - Shrewsbury bypasses and the A41 Whitchurch Bypass will be nearing readiness for tenders to be invited.

10.20 Schemes reaching advanced stages of preparation recently include the M5 "parallel widening" scheme for the section between Warndon and Strensham (which will bring the motorway up to dual 3-lane standard for its whole length between Carlisle and Exeter) on which a public inquiry took place in November 1989. Also at an advanced stage are Studley and Norton-Lenchwick Bypasses on the A435, the A5 Fazeley Two Gates Wilnecote improvement to take through traffic out of Tamworth and the Southam Bypass on the A423 in Warwickshire. Draft orders have now been published for this group.

10.21 Preferred routes were announced for the length of the proposed Birmingham Western Orbital Route between M5 and M54 and the related Kidderminster, Blakedown and Hagley Bypass. The private finance initiative for the Birmingham Northern Relief Road is moving into the tender stage following receipt of three successful pre-qualifying bids. These schemes will contribute to the Government's "Action for Cities" programme by relieving the pressures on the M5 and M6 through the West Midlands conurbation. Under that same initiative the Black Country Spine Road which is being prepared by Sandwell, Walsall and Wolverhampton MBCs with 100% grant funding is expected, subject to satisfactory completion of the statutory procedures and to final approvals, to start construction during the Summer of this year.

10.22 With the additions announced in the White Paper "Roads For Prosperity" notably widening of lengths of M6 and M42 as well as bypasses and other improvements on the A5, A38, A41, A45, A49, A435, A465, A500 and A523 the ongoing programme represents an investment of some £2 billion in the Region's motorway and trunk road network.

WEST MIDLANDS

Schemes costing over £1m

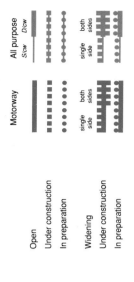

Motorway

Open

Under construction

In preparation

Widening

Under construction

In preparation

Region/County

All purpose
S/cw   D/cw

single   both
side   sides

single   both
side   sides

Widening

The symbol depicting widening schemes in preparation is not intended to indicate
which side or sides of the existing carriageway widening will take place.
Where schemes are under construction symbols are positioned on that side of the
carriageway where work is taking place.

The following abbreviations are used in some scheme names:
Bp-Bypass, Div-Diversion, Imp-Improvement, GSJ-Grade Separated Junction,
J-Junction.

*This map illustrates in diagrammatic form schemes in the trunk road programme and
does not necessarily indicate ultimate alignment.*

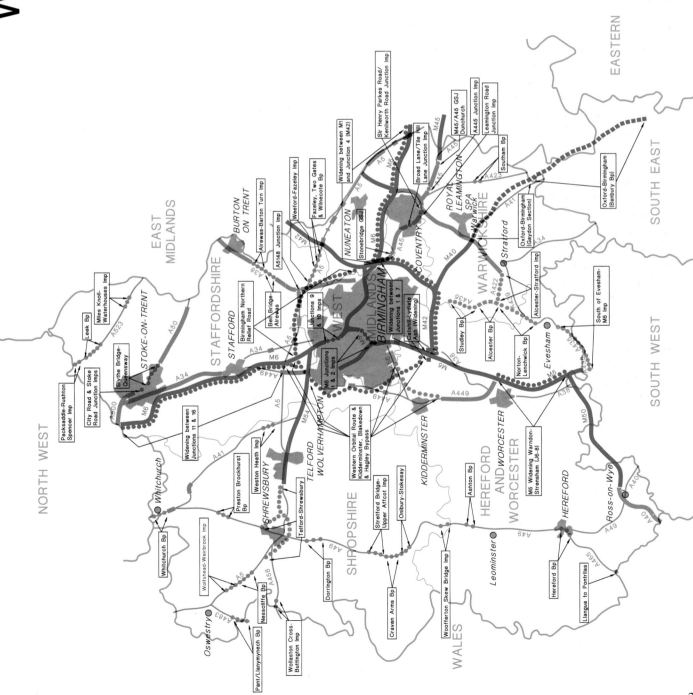

29

EAST MIDLANDS

10.23 The value of the East Midland Region forward programme was increased by £1.0 billion to a total of £1.5 billion with addition of schemes announced in "Roads For Prosperity". In addition, since April 1987, ten schemes have been completed and five contracts valued at £93 million are under construction. These include the construction of the final section of the M42/A42, Birmingham - Nottingham Route, which will link the Measham and Ashby Bypass (opened in August 1989) to the M1. Completion is planned for 1991. The East-West M1 - A1 Link through Northamptonshire is also under construction as is the A46 Newark Relief Road.

10.24 The M1 and the A1 are the principal North-South routes through the East Midlands. There are planned improvements to both. M1 is to be widened to dual 4-lane standard and on the A1 grade separation of three more major junctions is planned. A study will also consider the possibility of more comprehensive improvements to the A1, including upgrading to motorway status.

10.25 A decision on the A46 Leicester Western Bypass is expected soon. Further north the addition to the programme of proposed improvements to the A46 from Widmerpool to Lincoln will upgrade this strategic South-West/North-East Link between M1/M69, the A1 at Newark and through to Lincoln. Work continues on the planning of the A564 Stoke-Derby Route which will link the M6 to the M1 and in the East Midlands includes the Doveridge Bypass, Foston-Hatton-Hilton Bypass and the Derby Southern Bypass. Public inquiries are planned in 1990 for the latter two schemes.

10.26 Further major route improvements are planned for the A43 in Northamptonshire following completion of the Brackley and Towcester Bypasses. Work is due to start in 1990 on the Blisworth Bypass. Preparation continues on Silverstone Bypass, Whitfield Turn to Brackley Hatch, Moulton Bypass, the Moulton to Broughton Dualling, Kettering Northern Bypass and Geddington Bypass.

10.27 In Lincolnshire route improvements to the A16, east coast route, include South of Haven Bridge in Boston which is now open to traffic, Louth Bypass and the Boston - Algarkirk Diversion for which tenders have been invited and the 11 mile Spalding - Sutterton Improvement where orders have been published. The preferred route has been announced for the Stamford Relief Road and public consultation is complete for the Market Deeping and Deeping St James Bypass. Five smaller national schemes are also in preparation. On the important A17 which links Yorkshire and Humberside to East Anglia, the New Washway Road and Long Sutton-Sutton Bridge Bypass are open to traffic with the Fosdyke Bridge Improvement nearing completion. Orders have been published for the Wigtoft - Sutterton Bypass. The Leadenham Bypass is at public inquiry stage. Further improvements are planned between Leadenham and Sleaford, Sutterton and New Washway and from Sutton Bridge to the Norfolk county boundary.

10.28 The A6 which crosses the Region from South-East to North-West is undergoing comprehensive improvement between the M1 near Derby and the Northamptonshire-Bedfordshire boundary. Construction should start in 1990 on five sections of the route. These are the Quorn - Mountsorrel Bypass, the Market Harborough Bypass, the Burton Latimer Bypass, the Rothwell to Kettering Section and the Kettering Southern Bypass. The latter two are part of the M1 - A1 Link scheme. Several other improvements to the route are also planned, including an Eastern Bypass of Leicester and a Rushden and Higham Ferrers Bypass.

EAST MIDLANDS
Schemes costing over £1m

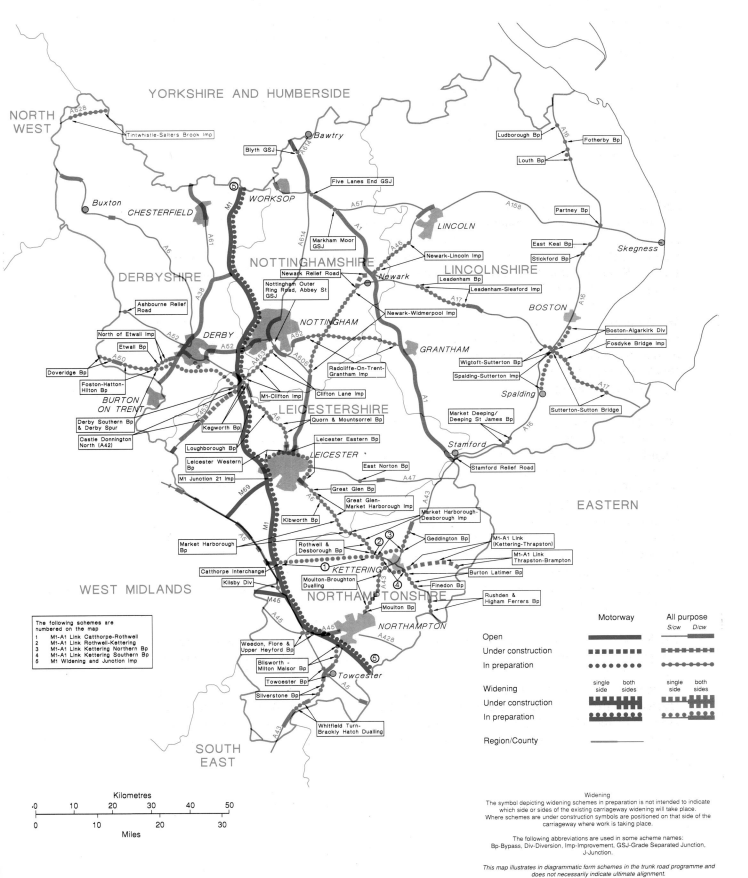

YORKSHIRE AND HUMBERSIDE

NORTH WEST

A628

Tintwhistle-Salters Brook Imp

Buxton

CHESTERFIELD

Blyth GSJ

Bawtry

A614

Five Lanes End GSJ

WORKSOP

A57

A1

M1

A61

Markham Moor GSJ

A614

LINCOLN

Newark-Lincoln Imp

Ludborough Bp

A16

Fotherby Bp

Louth Bp

Partney Bp

A158

Skegness

East Keal Bp

Stickford Bp

DERBYSHIRE

NOTTINGHAMSHIRE

A6

A38

Ashbourne Relief Road

North of Etwall Imp

A52

Etwall Bp

DERBY

A52

Doveridge Bp

A50

Foston-Hatton-Hilton Bp

BURTON ON TRENT

Derby Southern Bp & Derby Spur

Castle Donnington North (A42)

A453

Newark Relief Road

Nottingham Outer Ring Road, Abbey St GSJ

Newark

A46

LINCOLNSHIRE

Leadenham Bp

Leadenham-Sleaford Imp

A17

Newark-Widmerpool Imp

BOSTON

A16

NOTTINGHAM

A52

A606

GRANTHAM

Radcliffe-On-Trent-Grantham Imp

Boston-Algarkirk Div

Fosdyke Bridge Imp

Wigtoft-Sutterton Bp

Spalding-Sutterton Imp

M1-Clifton Imp

Clifton Lane Imp

Kegworth Bp

LEICESTERSHIRE

A6

Quorn & Mountsorrel Bp

A1

Spalding

Sutterton-Sutton Bridge

A17

Loughborough Bp

Leicester Western Bp

M1 Junction 21 Imp

Leicester Eastern Bp

LEICESTER

East Norton Bp

A47

Market Deeping/Deeping St James Bp

Stamford

A16

Stamford Relief Road

EASTERN

M69

A6

Great Glen Bp

Great Glen-Market Harborough Imp

A43

Market Harborough-Desborough Imp

Kibworth Bp

Geddington Bp

M1-A1 Link (Kettering-Thrapston)

M1-A1 Link Thrapston-Brampton

Market Harborough Bp

A6

M1

Rothwell & Desborough Bp

①

②

③

Burton Latimer Bp

Catthorpe Interchange

KETTERING

Finedon Bp

④

Kilsby Div

WEST MIDLANDS

M45

Moulton-Broughton Dualling

A43

NORTHAMPTONSHIRE

Rushden & Higham Ferrers Bp

A46

A45

Moulton Bp

NORTHAMPTON

A428

Weedon, Flore & Upper Heyford Bp

Blisworth - Milton Malsor Bp

⑤

Towcester Bp

Towcester

A5

Silverstone Bp

A43

Whitfield Turn-Brackly Hatch Dualling

SOUTH EAST

The following schemes are numbered on the map
1 M1-A1 Link Catthorpe-Rothwell
2 M1-A1 Link Rothwell-Kettering
3 M1-A1 Link Kettering Northern Bp
4 M1-A1 Link Kettering Southern Bp
5 M1 Widening and Junction Imp

	Motorway	All purpose
		S/cw D/cw
Open		
Under construction		
In preparation		
Widening	single side / both sides	single side / both sides
Under construction		
In preparation		
Region/County		

Kilometres
0 10 20 30 40 50
Miles
0 10 20 30

Widening
The symbol depicting widening schemes in preparation is not intended to indicate which side or sides of the existing carriageway widening will take place.
Where schemes are under construction symbols are positioned on that side of the carriageway where work is taking place.

The following abbreviations are used in some scheme names:
Bp-Bypass, Div-Diversion, Imp-Improvement, GSJ-Grade Separated Junction, J-Junction.

This map illustrates in diagrammatic form schemes in the trunk road programme and does not necessarily indicate ultimate alignment.

31

EASTERN

10.29 The Eastern Region is well served by a network of north-south motorway and trunk road routes radiating from M25, from the M40 in the west to the A13 in the east. It is proposed to widen over 170 miles of the most heavily-loaded sections of motorway, including lengths of the M1, the M40 from Junction 1A to Junction 5, and the whole of M25 in the Region. Thirty-six miles of new motorway are planned, including a new route from the M25 to Chelmsford bringing relief to both the north-east quadrant of M25 and the length of A12 northwards from the M25 to Chelmsford.

10.30 Much work is planned for A1. The A1(M) will be widened from Junction 1 to Junction 8, and from Junctions 9 to 10. The motorway is to be extended northwards from its present termination in the Letchworth/Baldock area to the proposed junction between the A1 and the M1 - A1 Link Road in Cambridgeshire; and the existing road will also be widened from there to Stamford. This programme of works will provide a minimum of dual 3-lane carriageways all the way from London, and will build on work already in hand to upgrade the existing road by improving junctions and closing central reserve gaps.

10.31 The M11 is to be improved from Junction 8 (Birchanger) to Junction 14 (Cambridge). With the improvement also proposed of the A604 from the northern end of M11, and with the M1 - A1 Link Road now under construction to the west of that, M11 will provide a very high standard alternative route to M1 and A1 from the south-east to destinations in the Midlands and North, as well as improving east-west routes through the Region. Also, in conjunction with the A11, now to be dualled all the way from M11 Junction 9 at Stump Cross to Norwich, the M11 will provide good communications to Norfolk.

10.32 The A5 is growing in strategic importance as an alternative to the M1. The planned programme provides for it to be dual carriageway throughout the Region.

10.33 Further strengthening of east-west routes is proposed. The east-west corridor north of London between the M40 and the ports of Felixstowe and Harwich is to be developed as a new trunk road, taking forward work already carried out by the local authorities. Some local authority schemes will continue, but new trunk road schemes will be promoted for four sections of the existing route. In addition to improving strategic links to the east coast ports, the route will enhance access to the expanding Stansted Airport. The A47 will become dual carriageway from the A1, to the west of Peterborough, to Norwich.

10.34 The total value of schemes for the Eastern Region is nearly £2.6 billion.

EASTERN

Schemes costing over £1m

The following schemes are numbered on the map

1. Little Brickhill-M1
2. Baldock-Alconbury
3. E/W Route A5-A1
4. M1 Junctions 10-15 Imp
5. M26 Widening
6. Buckinghamshire-Essex

Legend

	Motorway	All purpose
		Slow Dcw
both sides		
single side		

Open
Under construction
In preparation

Widening
Under construction
In preparation

Region/County

Widening
The symbol depicting widening schemes in preparation is not intended to indicate which side or sides of the existing carriageway widening will take place. Where schemes are under construction symbols are positioned on that side of the carriageway where work is taking place.

The following abbreviations are used in some scheme names:
Bp-Bypass, Div-Diversion, Imp-Improvement, GSJ-Grade Separated Junction, J-Junction.

This map illustrates in diagrammatic form schemes in the trunk road programme and does not necessarily indicate ultimate alignment.

Kilometres: 0 10 20 30 40 50
Miles: 0 10 20 30

Regions / Counties
EAST MIDLANDS
NORFOLK
SUFFOLK
CAMBRIDGESHIRE
BEDFORDSHIRE
BUCKINGHAMSHIRE
HERTFORDSHIRE
ESSEX
LONDON
SOUTH EAST

Towns
KING'S LYNN, PETERBOROUGH, NORWICH, GREAT YARMOUTH, LOWESTOFT, Thetford, Newmarket, CAMBRIDGE, Bury St. Edmunds, IPSWICH, FELIXSTOWE, HARWICH, COLCHESTER, CHELMSFORD, BASILDON, SOUTHEND-ON-SEA, Tilbury, Milton Keynes, BEDFORD, Dunstable, LUTON, Stevenage, Aylesbury, SLOUGH

Scheme labels
Acle Straight Imp
Garleston Relief Road
Lowestoft 2nd Harbour Crossing
Blofield-Acle
Scole-Norwich Imp
Saxmundham Bp Imp
Lowestoft 2nd Harbour Crossing
Saxmundham Bp-Lowestoft Widening
Saxmundham Imp
Wickham Market-Saxmundham Bp
Martlesham-Woodbridge Imp
Woodbridge-Wickham Market Imp
Beacon Hill (A45)-Scole Imp
Scole Bp
Norwich Southern Bp
Hardwick Roundabout-Easton
Narborough Bp
A134-Hardwick Roundabout
East Dereham-North Tuddenham Imps
Besthorpe-Wymondham Imp
Attleborough Bp Imp
Roudham Heath-Attleborough
Dickleburgh Bp
Fiveways Roundabout-Bridgham Heath
Brandon Creek-Southery
Thetford Bp
Red Lodge Bp
Newmarket-Red Lodge
Rookery Cross GSJ
Quarries Cross GSJ
Capel St. Mary GSJ
South of Four Sisters GSJ
E/W Route Braintree-A12
Hatfield Peverel-Marks Tey Widening
Chelmsford Bp Widening
Rayleigh Weir GSJ
M25-Rayleigh
Lakeside GSJ
Tilney High End-Sutton Bridge
Walpole Highway-Tilney High End Bp
Guyhirn Diversion
East of Thorney-East of Wisbech Imp
Cambridge-Ely Imp
M11-A10 Imp
Four Wentways-Newmarket Dualling
Four Wentways Junction Imp
Stump Cross-Four Wentways
Widening between Junctions 8-14
E/W Route Stansted-Braintree (100% grant)
Wadesmill, High Cross-Colliers End Bp
M25-Chelmsford
Peterborough-Stamford Imp
Castor-Ailsworth Bp
Eye Bp
Peterborough-East of Thorney Imp
Norman Cross Imp
Glatton GSJ
Bar Hill-M11/A1 Link Imp
Eaton Socon-Hardwick Imp
Tempsford GSJ
Langford Turn GSJ
Hay Lane-Buntingford Imp
E/W Route A1-Stansted
Junctions 9-10 Imp
Junctions 6-8 Imp
Junctions 1-6 Imp
Junction 5 North Facing Slip Roads
M25-Hoddesdon Imp
Alconbury-Peterborough Imp
Sutton-West of A1
Mt-A1 Link (Thrapston-Brampton)
South of Brampton Junction Imp
Great Barford Bp and extention to A1
Bedford Southern Bp
Barton-Le-Clay Bp
M1-Dunstable
Junctions 6A-10
Junctions 16-16 Imp
Wennington-Mar Dyke
Dartford-Thurrock Crossing Approach Roads
Clapham Bp
Bedford Western Bp
Lavendon Bp
Little Brickhill Bp
Sheep Lane GSJ
Junction 9 Climbing Lanes
Dunstable Bp
Aston Clinton Bp
Berkhamsted Bp
Kings Langley Bp
Junctions 1A-4 Widening
Junctions 4-6 Widening
Leighton Linslade Bp (100% grant)
E/W Route West of Aylesbury-Wing Bp

SOUTH WEST

10.35 The past two years have seen a significant improvement to the trunk road network in the South West Region. Some 20 major schemes have been completed including bypasses of Barnstaple, Bideford, Birdlip, Blackwater, Bridport, Dorchester, Ilminster, Okehampton, Saltash, Sparkford, Steeple Langford and Warminster as well as the final stages of the North Devon Link between Tiverton and Barnstaple. These schemes have eliminated most of the notorious bottlenecks in the Region, and led to improvements in the quality of life in the bypassed communities. The completion of the North Devon Link provides a new route from the national motorway network to North Devon and brings new opportunities to this area.

10.36 Steps being taken to provide a second Severn Bridge are referred to in paragraph 3.4 of this report. A number of new motorway schemes have been added to the national programme in the Bristol area. These include new links from M4 and M5 to the second Severn Bridge and longer term proposals for tackling congestion on sections of the M4 and M5 motorways.

10.37 Several schemes already in the programme have been extended to enable more effective solutions to be developed. These include the bypass of Stratton in Gloucestershire, which has been extended to bypass Cirencester, and the bypass of Brockworth, which has been extended to connect with Gloucester Northern Bypass.

10.38 A new major scheme, east of Bath, has been added to the programme, to link from the A46 at Batheaston to the A36 at Beckington. Further south, the proposed new northern bypass of Exeter from the M5 to the A30 west of the city, should help to ease congestion in the city and reduce traffic problems at Junction 30 on the M5.

10.39 Other schemes added will complete the improvement of the A303 to dual carriageway standard through Wiltshire, and improve four further stretches of the A30 in Cornwall. In addition it is proposed to bring the A380 between Exeter and Torbay into the trunk road network, to provide a new trunk route from Poole Harbour to the A31 and to improve the link from M5 to Avonmouth Docks, bypassing the community of Avonmouth, as a trunk road scheme.

10.40 Altogether there are over 60 schemes in the South West Region with a total value of over £1.1 billion.

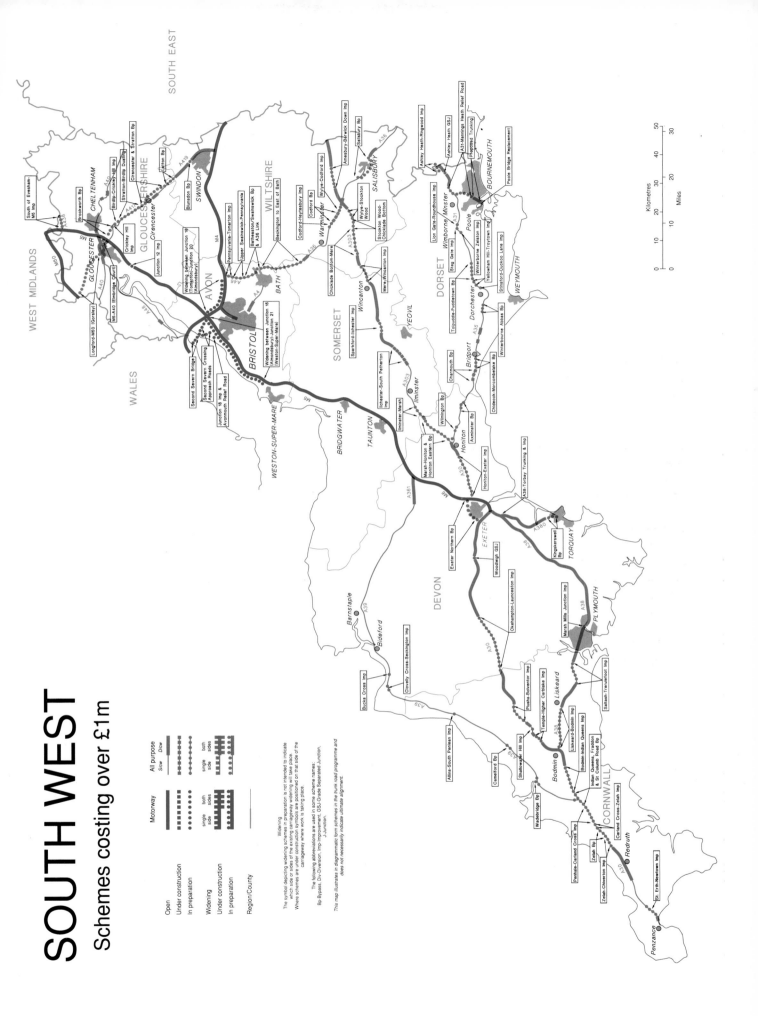

SOUTH WEST

Schemes costing over £1m

Motorway

- Open
- Under construction
- In preparation

All purpose

Slow Dfow

- Open
- Under construction
- In preparation

Widening

- Under construction
  - single both side sides
- In preparation
  - single both side sides

— Region/County

The symbol depicting widening schemes in preparation is not intended to indicate which side or sides of the existing carriageway widening will take place. Where schemes are under construction symbols are positioned on that side of the carriageway where work is taking place.

The following abbreviations are used in some scheme names:
Bp–Bypass, Div–Diversion, Imp–Improvement, GSJ–Grade Separated Junction, J–Junction.

This map illustrates in diagrammatic form schemes in the trunk road programme and does not necessarily indicate ultimate alignment.

Kilometres / Miles

35

SOUTH EAST

10.41 New schemes announced in "Roads For Prosperity" doubled the roads programme in the South East, with planned expenditure now totalling over £2 billion. Approximately half of this is for widening of congested sections of existing motorways and new motorway construction. The remainder is for improvements to the all-purpose trunk road network.

10.42 The programme already included completion of the M3, M20 and M40 routes, to which priority continues to be given, together with some motorway widening, and major schemes on most of the Region's all-purpose trunk roads.

10.43 About two thirds of the planned additional expenditure will go to further schemes for tackling motorway congestion, including some £500 million for widening all the present dual 3-lane sections of the M25 within the Region to dual 4-lane standard. In addition the capacity of the Thames Crossing at Dartford is being doubled by the privately financed provision of a 4-lane bridge. The other new widening proposals cover sections of the M3 and M23 in Surrey, M4 in Berkshire and Wiltshire, and M2 and M20 in Kent. On all but M23, these augment previously programmed schemes. Programmed schemes bring actual or planned dual 4-lane provision on the eastern length of M4 to a continuous 59 miles, from the Heathrow Spur to Swindon.

10.44 Good progress is being made on the four previously programmed schemes for completing high standard improvement of M20/A20 as the main road artery between M25/M26 and the Channel Tunnel, Folkestone and Dover. The aim remains to have all in place by the time the Tunnel opens, subject to completion of the outstanding statutory procedures.

10.45 Routes to the ports figure prominently in the Region's planned improvements to all-purpose trunk roads. Together with the final sections of M3 and M40, the A34 Newbury Bypass will complete an important connection between the West Midlands and the South Coast ports. Others include schemes on the A3 London-Portsmouth road which is being progressively improved, on the most congested sections of the A2/M2 route in Kent, and on the A249 to Sheerness. Proposals for A249, the Isle of Sheppey's only road link, include a new crossing of the Swale estuary.

10.46 With schemes completed or under construction and the further schemes now programmed, the A27/A259 South Coast trunk route is being progressively improved over almost its entire length between Portsmouth and Folkestone. Other all-purpose roads for which major improvement is planned include A23, to complete a high standard M23/A23 route between the M25 and Brighton; A21 in Kent and East Sussex; A31 between the M27 and Ringwood; A339 between Basingstoke and Newbury; the Oxfordshire length of A420; and A40 in the Oxford area. As well as benefiting road users, a great many of the Region's schemes will provide considerable relief to residents by bypassing communities.

10.47 Looking further ahead beyond the present programme, there are to be scheme identification studies on motorways and trunk roads in Kent and East Sussex, and another which has already been put in hand in the Southampton area. Studies will also be commissioned into the major strategic issues of possible need for a new East-West route between Kent and Hampshire, a Lower Thames Crossing between Kent and Essex and an M3 - M40 link between Surrey and Buckinghamshire.

SOUTH EAST

Schemes costing over £1m

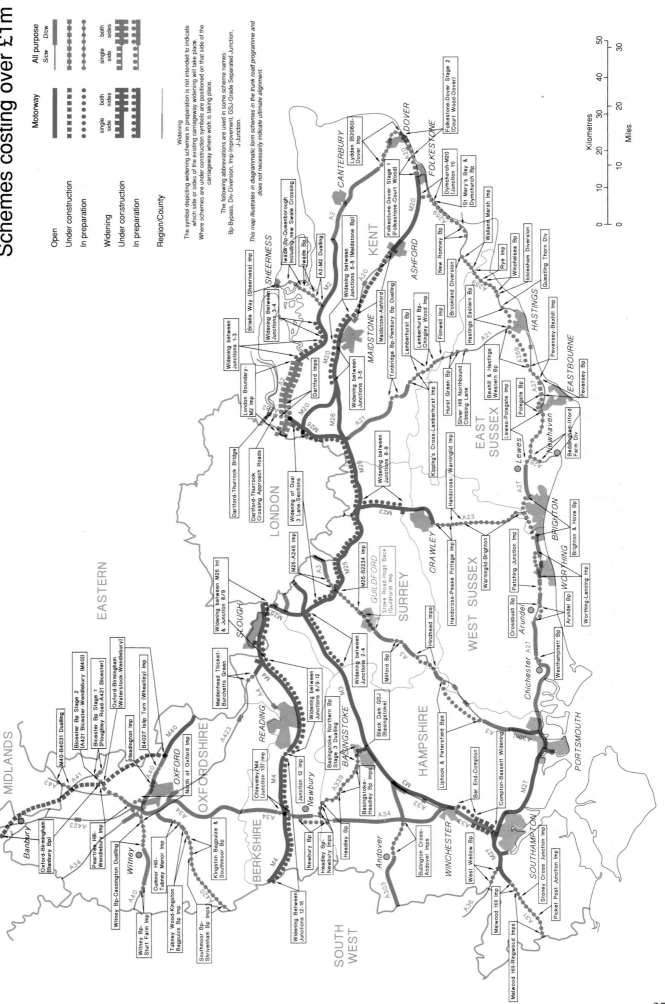

Motorway

Open	single side	both sides
Under construction		
In preparation		

Widening
Under construction
In preparation

All purpose
Slow / D/cw

single side	both sides	

Region/County

Widening
The symbol depicting widening schemes in preparation is not intended to indicate which side or sides of the existing carriageway widening will take place. Where schemes are under construction symbols are positioned on that side of the carriageway where work is taking place.

The following abbreviations are used in some scheme names:
Bp-Bypass, Div-Diversion, Imp-Improvement, GSJ-Grade Separated Junction, J-Junction.

This map illustrates the diagrammatic form schemes in the trunk road programme and does not necessarily indicate ultimate alignment.

11 LONDON

11.1 It is not the Government's policy to encourage additional car commuting into central London. In fact nearly 85 per cent of people commuting to central London during the peak hours of 7.00 to 10.00 use public transport. It is the Government's policy to improve public transport in London. In November 1989 the Secretary of State for Transport announced a major addition to the London Underground with the proposed extension of the Jubilee Line from Green Park to Docklands via Waterloo. It is estimated that this project will cost £1 billion with some of the money being provided by private developers.

11.2 The Government has considered the use of road pricing to reduce traffic congestion on the capital's roads, but has ruled it out for the foreseeable future. It believes that such a solution would present formidable technical and administrative problems, particularly in a city as large and complex as London.

11.3 Particular emphasis is being given to making the most effective use of existing road space. There are, for example, continuing programmes to eliminate stress points and bottlenecks on London's trunk roads and to use the latest technology to improve London's traffic light systems. By the end of 1993, the SCOOT system, which co-ordinates traffic lights and adjusts their timings automatically to changing traffic conditions, will be installed at 800 signals. New systems to control traffic are being installed in East London and on the North Circular Road; and proposals have been developed for modernising the signing on the Primary Route Network.

11.4 Improvements to London's trunk road network, along with extensive investment in better public transport, are making an important contribution to dealing with the capital's transport problems. There has been continuing progress in taking forward the programme of London schemes with emphasis on upgrading the A406 North Circular Road, the A40 serving west London, and the A13 providing access from the M25 to Docklands and East London. Major schemes completed in the past two years have been the A20 Sidcup Bypass and the South Woodford to Barking Relief Road, which extends the North Circular Road to the A13. Both schemes have been very succesful in relieving congestion and the local road network in the corridors they serve. The A2 Rochester Way Relief Road, which was opened in April 1988 has eased the flow of traffic proceeding to the River Thames Crossing at Blackwall Tunnel and has been successful in reducing flows and accidents on other radial routes.

11.5 Six schemes are due to be completed in the next two years: the A406 North Circular Road junction improvement with Great Cambridge Road (A10), the Chingford Road to Hale End Road improvement, the A40 Swakeleys Road Junction Improvement in Hillingdon, the A23 Waddon Marsh Bridge Bridge Improvement in Croydon and the A13 Leamouth and West India Dock Road junction improvements.

11.6 Public inquiries have been held into five major junction improvement schemes: Regent's Park Road, Silver Street and Dysons Road on the North Circular Road, and the Western Circus and Gypsy Corner Junction Improvements on the A40. Decisions on all five are expected soon.

11.7 Public consultation was held in 1989 on the A23 Coulsdon Inner Relief Road and the Western Environmental Improvement Route (WEIR). The Coulsdon Inner Relief Road will take through traffic out of the town centre and improve conditions for local residents. The purpose of WEIR is to relieve adjoining areas of Hammersmith and Kensington of traffic providing the opportunity for traffic management schemes and associated environmental improvements in local shopping and residential roads.

11.8 The preferred scheme for improvements at the A13/A117 junction will be announced soon.

Docklands

11.9   The success of the Government's policies for regenerating Docklands in the form of increased employment and population have exceeded earlier expectations. Trunk road improvements are making an important contribution to access to Docklands with a programme of over £450 million comprising twelve major schemes. These schemes complement those for new roads within Docklands being undertaken by the London Docklands Development Corporation.

East London River Crossing

11.10 The line of the East London River Crossing to link the South Woodford to Barking Relief Road with the A2 at Falconwood has been established following a public inquiry extending over fifteen months. However it is now proposed to change the form of the bridge from a cable stayed to box girder structure. This would keep open options for the future use of London City Airport. Joint public inquiries will be held into the revised bridge proposals and a planning application to allow other types of aircraft to use the airport. The revised bridge proposals would also enable the bridge to be built with full width dual 3-lanes for the additional traffic now expected to use it as a result of the success of Docklands.

Blackwall Tunnel

11.11 The Blackwall Tunnel comprises two tunnels. The northbound tunnel was opened over 100 years ago and the southbound tunnel 20 years ago. The northbound tunnel was not designed with modern traffic requirements in mind and generally there is an increasing problem of traffic congestion at this Thames crossing point. It is therefore proposed to construct an additional tunnel parallel to the existing southbound tunnel and to convert the existing northbound tunnel for two-way local light vehicle traffic between the Greenwich Peninsula and Docklands. This will entail building a spur off the northbound tunnel into the Isle of Dogs.

London Assessment Studies

11.12 Consultants were commissioned in 1984 to undertake major studies of four areas of the capital with severe transport-related problems: East London, South London, the South Circular Road Corridor and West London. Reports on the second stage of the studies were published in December 1989. The objectives of these studies, which were agreed with the local authorities, were to:

- promote accessibility;

- support employment, economic growth and regeneration;

- develop an efficient transport system;

- improve the environment and

- enhance safety for travellers.

These objectives include dealing more efficiently with existing traffic, relieving unsuitable residential roads and shopping streets, and enabling pedestrians and cyclists to move more freely and in safety. The consultants looked at a wide range of options including public transport improvements and better traffic management as well as road improvements. The Government has indicated the options suggested by the consultants which it is to consider further and those it has ruled out.

Other studies

11.13 The Heathrow Access and South West London Quadrant Study (HASQUAD) is now entering its second stage looking for solutions to the problems of orbital movement in this part of West London. Stage I collected data relevant to travel in the area and identified the problems associated with orbital movements. Discussions are being held with BAA plc on the potential trunk road implications of the possible further expansion of Heathrow Airport. A report will be made towards the middle of the year on the M4/A4 corridor study, which is aimed at improving the reliability of journey times in this corridor within the M25.

11.14 In addition to the proposed new tunnel at Blackwall announced in December 1989 a review of the need for additional river crossing capacity between Blackwall and Tower Bridge is to be commissioned.

11.15 A programme of further radical and coherent traffic management initiatives was announced in December 1989. It includes proposals to improve traffic conditions on the main routes for longer distance traffic in London by developing a 300 mile priority network of "red routes", where special restrictions on stopping and parking will apply, under the control of a Traffic Director. It also includes proposals for a more effective system of parking controls, by confining yellow lines strictly to places where they are needed, increasing the fixed penalty levels for illegal parking and vigorous enforcement of the controls. Comments on the proposals have been invited by 28 February 1990.

LONDON

Schemes costing over £1m

This map illustrates in diagrammatic form schemes in the trunk road programme and does not necessarily indicate ultimate alignment.

	Motorway	All purpose
		S/cw D/cw
Open		
Under construction		
In preparation		
	single side both sides	single side both sides
Widening		
Under construction		
In preparation		
Region/County		

MOTORWAYS

1 M1/A1 Scratchwood Link
2 M1 Junction 1 Improvement
3 M4 Junction 4 and 4A Improvement

ALL PURPOSE ROADS

4 Gallows Corner Intersection Improvement
5 Whalebone Lane Junction Improvement
6 Thames Avenue - Wennington
7 East London River Crossing
8 Heathway - Ballards Road Junction Improvements
9 Movers Lane Junction Improvement
10 A13/A117 Junction Improvement
11 A13/A112 Prince Regent Lane Junction
12 Ironbridge Junction Improvement
13 Leamouth Junction Interim Scheme
14 A102 Blackwall Tunnel Third Bore
15 Blackwall Tunnel/Cotton Street Junction & Tunnel Spur & Blackwall Junction Interim Scheme
16 West India Dock Road Junction Improvement & West India Dock Road Interim Junction Improvement
17 Butcher Row Junction Improvement
18 Hackney Wick - M11 Link
19 Chingford Road - Hale End Road
20 Dysons Road - Hall Lane
21 East of Silver Street - A1010
22 Great Cambridge Road (A10) Junction Improvement
23 Bounds Green - Green Lanes Improvement
24 Falloden Way - Finchley High Road
25 Regents Park Road Junction Improvement
26 Golders Green Road Junction Improvement
27 Ironbridge - Neasden Improvement
28 Hanger Lane - Harrow Road
29 Long Lane-West End Road
30 Long Lane Junction Improvement
31 Swakeleys Road Junction Improvement
32 Waggoner's Corner (A4/A312) Junction Improvement
33 Henleys Corner (A4/A30) Junction Improvement
34 Popes Lane - Western Avenue
35 Gipsy Corner Junction Improvement
36 Western Circus Junction Improvement
37 Western Environmental Improvement Route
38 Robin Hood Gate Junction - Roehampton Vale Improvement
39 Hook Interchange Improvement
40 Coulsdon Inner Relief Road
41 Waddon Marsh Bridge
42 Catford Town Centre Improvement
43 Kidbrooke Park Road Interchange

EASTERN

SOUTH EAST

Widening

The symbol depicting widening schemes in preparation is not intended to indicate which side or sides of the existing carriageway widening will take place.
Where schemes are under construction symbols are positioned on that side of the carriageway where work is taking place.

41

REFERENCES

1. National Road Traffic Forecasts (Great Britain) 1989, HMSO 1989.

2. National Audit Office Report on National Energy Efficiency HC547 Session 1988-89, HMSO 1989.

3. M25 Review Summary Report, Rendel, Palmer and Tritton, HMSO 1989.

ANNEX A
TRUNK ROAD SCHEME PREPARATION

The diagram below sets out the key preparation stages for a trunk road scheme and indicates the range of time that may be taken from one stage to the next, depending on its size, complexity and the extent of objections. For each scheme in Table 3 the next key preparation stage is shown and the target date by when it is expected to be reached. An expected start of works date is indicated for those schemes where the main Highways Act orders have been made.

KEY PREPARATION STAGES FOR TRUNK ROAD SCHEME

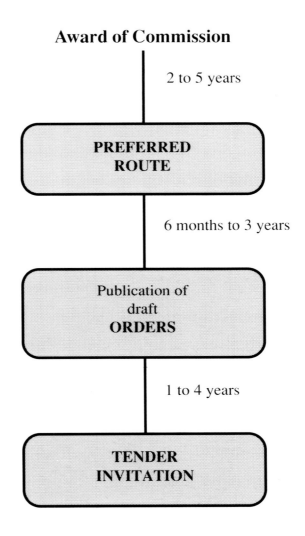

Award of Commission

2 to 5 years

PREFERRED ROUTE

6 months to 3 years

Publication of draft **ORDERS**

1 to 4 years

TENDER INVITATION

The public are usually consulted about road proposals. Their comments are taken into account in selecting a preferred route. Preparation of draft orders to authorise the scheme then begins. When the orders are published, they are open to objections and representations; generally if objections cannot be resolved a public inquiry is convened before an independent inspector nominated by the Lord Chancellor and appointed by the Secretary of State for the Environment and the Secretary of State for Transport acting jointly. About two thirds of inquiries take ten working days or less, but those for large or controversial schemes take longer (to date the longest inquiry has been spread over a period of fifteen months). On completion of an inquiry the inspector prepares his report and presents it to the Secretaries of State. They consider the inspector's recommendations and come to a joint decision on whether the scheme should go ahead with or without modifications. Once the orders have been made the way is open for detailed design to be completed. Tenders are then invited. Once a contract has been awarded construction can begin.

TABLE 1: NATIONAL TRUNK ROAD PROGRAMME SCHEMES COMPLETED BETWEEN 25 APRIL 1987 AND 31 DECEMBER 1989

Route Number	Scheme	Standard	Works Cost (£ million Outturn prices)	Length (Miles)	Date of Completion
M1	Junction 34 North & South Roundabout Improvements, Sheffield MB	--	1.2	--	September 1989
M5	Widening Warndon -- Rashwood, Hereford & Worcester	D3	18.5	5.2	November 1988
M25	Widening between Junctions 11 & 13, Surrey	D4	26.1	5.8	October 1989
M40	Warwick North, Warwickshire	D3	26.7	6.3	December 1989
M40	Warwick South, Warwickshire	D3	22.4	4.7	December 1989
M62	Westbound Climbing Lane (West of Junction 25), Kirklees MB	--	3.5	3.1	January 1989
M62	Eastbound Climbing Lane between Junctions 21 -- 22, Rochdale MB	D4	3.8	3.8	December 1988
M63	Stages 1&2 Widening, Salford MB, Trafford MB	D3	20.4	1.7	December 1988
M63	Stage 3 Widening, Trafford MB	D3	3.6	1.1	November 1987
M63/M66	Portwood -- Denton, Stockport MB, Tameside MB	D3/D2	50.1	5.0	April 1989
A1	A1 Clifton -- Stannington, Northumberland	D2	6.4	2.5	October 1987
A1	Dishforth Interchange, N. Yorkshire	D2	8.3	1.0	October 1989
A1	Baldersby Grade Separated Junction, N. Yorkshire	D2	2.8	--	May 1987
A1	Wetherby Bypass, Leeds MB	D2	11.5	1.5	July 1988
A2	Rochester Way Relief Rd, LB Greenwich	D2	61.0	3.5	March 1988
A2	Barham Crossroads Grade Separated Junction, Kent	--	2.3	--	June 1987
A3	Compton -- Shackleford Improvement, Surrey	D2	9.7	2.7	December 1989
A6	Chapel-en-le-Frith & Whaley Bridge Bypass, Derbyshire	D2/S	37.5	4.4	August 1987
A10	Melbourn Bypass, Cambridgeshire	S	4.2	3.3	July 1988
A10	Buntingford Bypass, Hertfordshire	S	5.0	3.0	June 1987
A11	Wymondham -- Cringleford, Norfolk	D2	8.4	5.2	November 1987
A12	Martlesham Bypass, Suffolk	D2	7.1	1.9	November 1987
A16	Diversion South of Haven Bridge, Lincolnshire	S	2.8	0.9	August 1989
A17	New Washway Road, Lincolnshire	S	3.9	2.8	August 1988
A17	Long Sutton -- Sutton Bridge Bypass, Lincolnshire	S	11.5	7.3	October 1989
A17	Cross Keys Bridge Refurbishment, Lincolnshire	--	3.7	--	October 1989

TABLE 1: NATIONAL TRUNK ROAD PROGRAMME SCHEMES COMPLETED BETWEEN 25 APRIL 1987 AND 31 DECEMBER 1989

Route Number	Scheme	Standard	Works Cost (£ million Outturn prices)	Length (Miles)	Date of Completion
A19	Riccall and Barlby Bypass, N. Yorkshire	S	5.4	4.6	October 1987
A20	Sidcup Bypass, LB Bexley	D2/D3	37.2	3.8	November 1987
A21	Pembury Bypass, Kent	D2	10.3	2.9	May 1988
A21	Robertsbridge Bypass, E. Sussex	S	4.4	1.2	November 1989
A27	Fontwell Bypass, W. Sussex	D2	4.9	2.1	August 1988
A27	Havant Bypass -- Chichester Bypass, Hampshire, W. Sussex	D2	29.3	8.6	August 1988
A30	Exeter -- Okehampton Stage 3, Devon	D2	16.2	5.4	July 1987
A30	Okehampton Bypass, Devon	D2	22.3	5.5	July 1988
A30	Blackwater Bypass, Cornwall	D2	5.2	2.2	July 1988
A30	Launceston -- Plusha Improvement, Cornwall	D2	10.5	5.9	December 1989
A34	Hanford Grade Separated Junction, Staffordshire	--	4.3	--	February 1989
A34	Whitway Diversion, Hampshire	D2	7.6	3.8	February 1989
A35	Dorchester Bypass, Dorset	S	9.2	3.9	October 1988
A35	Bridport Link Road, Dorset	S	5.9	1.8	July 1988
A36	Beckington Bypass, Wiltshire	D2/S	4.6	2.1	November 1989
A36	Warminster Bypass, Wiltshire	S	12.0	6.1	October 1988
A36	Steeple Langford Bypass, Wiltshire	S	1.5	1.4	January 1989
A38	Hilliards Cross Grade Separated Junction, Staffordshire	--	1.7	--	December 1987
A38	Belvedere Cross Grade Separated Junction, Devon	--	0.9	--	May 1987
A38	Saltash Bypass, Cornwall	D2/S	13.6	2.4	September 1988
A39	Barnstaple Bypass, Devon	S	20.5	9.3	July 1989
A39	Bideford Bypass, Devon	S	18.3	5.1	May 1987
A42	Measham & Ashby Bypass, Leicestershire	D2	33.6	6.4	August 1989
A43	Towcester Bypass, Northamptonshire	D2	5.4	3.4	February 1988
A43	Brackley Bypass, Northamptonshire	D2	8.5	4.5	August 1987
A46	Coventry Eastern Bypass, Coventry MB, Warwickshire	D2	21.0	5.1	May 1989
A47	Acle Bypass, Norfolk	D2	7.1	2.5	March 1989
A47	Postwick -- Blofield Dualling, Norfolk	D2	1.2	1.1	November 1987
A47	Peterborough Longthorpe Grade Separated Junction, Cambridgeshire	--	1.1	--	December 1987
A47	Wardley Hill Improvement, Leicestershire	S	1.9	2.0	October 1987

TABLE 1: NATIONAL TRUNK ROAD PROGRAMME SCHEMES COMPLETED BETWEEN 25 APRIL 1987 AND 31 DECEMBER 1989

Route Number	Scheme	Standard	Works Cost (£ million Outturn prices)	Length (Miles)	Date of Completion
A48	Chepstow Inner Relief Road, Gloucestershire	S	8.0	1.0	January 1988
A49	Prees Bypass, Shropshire	S	1.3	2.1	August 1988
A49	Leominster Bypass, Hereford & Worcester	S	9.0	4.0	November 1988
A52	Bottesford Bypass, Leicestershire	S	3.4	3.2	February 1989
A64	Seamer & Crossgates Bypass, N. Yorkshire	S	6.6	2.2	February 1988
A65	Settle & Giggleswick Bypass, N. Yorkshire	S	8.5	3.9	December 1988
A69	Horsley -- Corbridge Improvement, Northumberland	D2	3.4	2.5	December 1988
A69	Eighton Lodge Junction Improvement, Tyne & Wear	D2	6.0	1.2	December 1987
A303	Furze Hedge Grade Separated Junction, Wiltshire	--	0.7	--	July 1987
A303	Thruxton -- Amesbury, Hampshire	D2	11.2	6.0	October 1988
A303	Sparkford Bypass, Somerset	D2	9.8	3.2	October 1989
A303	Ilminster Bypass, Somerset	S	19.7	8.7	July 1988
A361	North Devon Link Stage 2A, Devon	S	27.6	15.1	November 1988
A361	North Devon Link Stage 2B, Devon	S	25.3	11.3	July 1989
A406	South Woodford -- Barking Relief Road, LBs Barking & Dagenham, Newham, Redbridge	D3	86.0	6.5	December 1987
A417	Birdlip Bypass, Gloucestershire	S	2.4	1.7	December 1988
A419	Blunsdon -- Cricklade Improvement, Wiltshire	D2	2.7	2.4	June 1988
A422	Stratford Northern Bypass, Warwickshire	D2/S	11.6	7.0	June 1987
A435	Evesham Bypass, Hereford & Worcester	S	7.3	4.0	July 1987
A435	Sedgeberrow Bypass, Hereford & Worcester	S	1.3	1.4	May 1989
A483	Chester Southerly Bypass -- Welsh Border, Cheshire	D2	4.7	2.4	January 1989
A500	Barthomley Link -- M6, Cheshire	S	6.9	3.4	July 1987
A565	Derby Road Improvement, Sefton MB	D2	2.1	0.7	October 1989
A595	Thursby Bypass, Cumbria	S	1.5	1.1	August 1987
A616	Stocksbridge -- M1, Barnsley MB, Sheffield MB	S	21.4	7.5	May 1988
A629	Airedale Route Section 1 (Kildwick -- Beechcliffe), Bradford MB	D2	17.2	4.6	August 1988
A650	Airedale Route Section 2 (Victoria Park -- Crossflatts), Bradford MB	D2	14.0	2.2	October 1988

TABLE 2: NATIONAL TRUNK ROAD PROGRAMME SCHEMES UNDER CONSTRUCTION AT 1 JANUARY 1990

Route Number	Scheme	Standard	Works Cost (£ million Current prices)	Length (Miles)	Expected Completion Date
M3	Compton -- Bassett Widening, Hampshire	D3	49.9	5.6	September 1991
M5	Catshill -- Lydiate Ash (Widening), Hereford & Worcester.	D3/D2	21.2	3.6	March 1990
M20	Maidstone -- Ashford (Contract 1), Kent	D3	45.7	7.5	April 1991
M20	Maidstone -- Ashford (Contract 2), Kent	D3	32.0	6.7	July 1991
M40	Gaydon Section, Warwickshire	D3	34.0	7.5	March 1991
M40	Banbury Bypass Section 1, Oxfordshire	D3	24.2	5.4	December 1990
M40	Banbury Bypass Section 2, Oxfordshire	D3	17.9	4.6	June 1990
M40	Banbury Bypass Section 3, Oxfordshire	D3	52.5	7.6	November 1990
M40	Banbury Bypass Section 4, Warwickshire, Oxfordshire	D3	51.7	9.9	September 1990
M40	Waterstock -- Wendlebury, Oxfordshire, Buckinghamshire	D3	77.2	12.6	March 1991
M63	Stage 4 widening, Trafford MB	D3	20.8	2.1	January 1990
A1	Newcastle Western Bypass, Northumberland, Tyne & Wear	D3/D2	76.6	6.9	December 1990
A2	London Boundary -- M2 Improvement, Kent	D3	10.9	12.5	In stages to September 1991
A6	Barton-Le-Clay Bypass, Bedfordshire	D2	9.4	1.3	December 1990
A11	Thetford Bypass, Norfolk	D2	13.0	4.7	November 1990
A13	Lakeside Grade Separated Junction, Essex	--	4.8	--	September 1990
A14	M1 - A1 Link, Kettering -- Thrapston Section, Northamptonshire	D2	25.7	6.5	May 1991
A14	M1 - A1 Link Thrapston -- Brampton (A), Northamptonshire, Cambridgeshire	D2	19.6	6.8	May 1991
A17	Fosdyke Bridge Improvement, Lincolnshire	S	2.9	--	April 1990
A19	Peterlee Grade Separated Junction, Durham	--	4.5	1.0	May 1990
A23	Waddon Marsh Bridge, LB Croydon	--	4.0	--	December 1990
A27	Pevensey Bypass, E. Sussex	S	8.8	3.3	August 1991
A27	Brighton & Hove Bypass, (Dyke Road -- Patcham), E. Sussex	D3	20.7	1.1	July 1991
A35	Charmouth Bypass, Dorset	S	13.0	2.7	July 1990
A36	Codford Bypass, Wiltshire	S	3.1	1.7	August 1990
A40	Swakeleys Road Junction Improvement, L B Hillingdon	--	13.0	--	February 1990

TABLE 2:   NATIONAL TRUNK ROAD PROGRAMME SCHEMES UNDER CONSTRUCTION AT 1 JANUARY 1990

Route Number	Scheme	Standard	Works Cost (£ million Current prices)	Length (Miles)	Expected Completion Date
A41	Chester Improvement, Cheshire	D2	21.2	3.0	September 1991
A41	Bicester Bypass Stage 1 (Ploughley Road -- A421 Bicester), Oxfordshire	S	5.7	1.8	January 1991
A42	Castle Donington North Contract 1, Leicestershire	D2	24.6	6.5	May 1991
A43	Peartree Hill -- Wendlebury Improvement, Oxfordshire	D2	24.6	6.2	June 1990
A46	Newark Relief Road, Nottinghamshire	S	34.0	5.8	October 1990
A47	Guyhirn Diversion, Cambridgeshire	S	5.0	0.8	March 1991
A52	Nottingham Outer Ring Road, Abbey Street Grade Separated Junction, Nottinghamshire	--	5.5	--	June 1990
A65	Addingham Bypass, Bradford MB	S	3.7	2.5	January 1991
A66	Stockton Racecourse Grade Separated Junction, Cleveland	--	7.4	--	November 1990
A69	Brampton Bypass, Cumbria	S	5.0	3.4	March 1991
A127	Rayleigh Weir Grade Separated Junction, Essex	--	12.4	--	December 1991
A282	Dartford - Thurrock Bridge, Kent, Essex	D4	Privately Financed	1.7	Summer 1991
A282	Dartford - Thurrock Crossing, Approach Roads, Kent	D4	37.4	2.3	Summer 1991
A303	Ilchester -- South Petherton Improvement, Somerset	D2	17.3	4.5	June 1991
A406	Chingford Road -- Hale End Road, LB Waltham Forest	D3	80.0	1.3	December 1991
A406	Great Cambridge Road Grade Separated Junction, LB Enfield	--	22.3	--	January 1990
A435	Alcester Bypass, Warwickshire	D2/S	15.0	3.8	November 1990
A500	Nantwich Bypass, Cheshire	S	5.6	2.2	October 1990
A696	Woolsington Bypass, Newcastle MB	D2	12.6	3.0	November 1990

TABLE 3: NATIONAL TRUNK ROAD PROGRAMME SCHEMES IN PREPARATION AT 1 JANUARY 1990

Route Number	Scheme	Proposed Standard	Estimated Works Cost (£ million November 87 prices)	Approximate Length (Miles)	Next Key Preparation Stage and Target Date *	Start of Works Date
MOTORWAY SCHEMES						
	Greater Manchester Western & Northern Relief Road (M6 -- M56 Section), Cheshire	D3	45.0	5.0	Preferred Route, Summer 1990	--
	Greater Manchester Western & Northern Relief Road (M56 -- M62 Section), Trafford MB, Salford MB, Cheshire	D3	105.0	6.0	Preferred Route, Winter 1991/92	--
	Greater Manchester Western & Northern Relief Road (M62 -- M66 Section), Salford MB, Bury MB	D3	150.0	9.0	Preferred Route, Winter 1991/92	--
	M1 - A1 Link Road (Belle Isle -- Hook Moor), Leeds MB	D3	100.0	9.8	Preferred Route, Summer 1990	--
	Birmingham Northern Relief Road, Warwickshire, Staffordshire, Walsall MB, Birmingham MB	--	--	30.0	Tenders to be invited for private finance, Spring 1990	--
	Western Orbital Route and Kidderminster, Blakedown & Hagley Bypass, Hereford & Worcester, Staffordshire	D4/ D3/D2	307.0	43.4	Orders, Summer 1990	--
M1/M62	Lofthouse Interchange Diversion, Leeds MB	D2	10.0	3.0	Preferred Route, Autumn 1991	--
M1	Widening between Junctions 30 & 32, Rotherham MB	D4	48.0	7.0	Preferred Route, 1992	--
M1	Widening between Junctions 15 & 30, Derbyshire, Nottinghamshire, Leicestershire, Northamptonshire	D4	794.0	91.0	Preferred Route, 1992	--
M1	Junction 21 Improvement, Leicestershire	--	10.2	--	Preferred Route, 1993	--
M1	Widening between Junctions 10 & 15, Bedfordshire, Buckinghamshire, Northamptonshire	D4	128.0	24.0	Preferred Route, 1992	--
M1	Widening between Junctions 6A & 10, Hertfordshire, Bedfordshire	D4	25.0	12.0	Preferred Route, 1992	--
M1	Junction 9 Climbing Lanes, Hertfordshire	D4	10.1	2.9	Orders, Spring 1990	--
M1	Junction 1 Improvement, LB Barnet	D2	2.9	--	Preferred Route, Autumn 1990	--
M2	Widening between Junctions 1 & 3, Kent	D3	30.0	5.0	Preferred Route, Winter 1991/92	--
M2	Widening between Junctions 3 & 4, Kent	D3	18.0	4.0	Preferred Route, Winter 1991/92	--

TABLE 3: NATIONAL TRUNK ROAD PROGRAMME SCHEMES IN PREPARATION AT 1 JANUARY 1990

Route Number	Scheme	Proposed Standard	Estimated Works Cost (£ million November 87 prices)	Approximate Length (Miles)	Next Key Preparation Stage and Target Date *	Start of Works Date
M3	Widening between Junctions 2 & 4, Surrey, Hampshire	D4	41.3	11.1	Preferred Route, Spring 1991	
M3	Bar End -- Compton, Hampshire	D3	36.0	3.7	Tender Invitation, Summer 1991	--
M4	Junction 4 & 4A Improvement, LB Hillingdon	--	12.4	--	Preferred Route, Autumn 1990	--
M4	Widening between M25 Interchange & Junction 8/9, Berkshire, Buckinghamshire	D4	60.9	8.7	Preferred Route, Autumn 1991	--
M4	Widening between Junctions 8/9 & 12, Berkshire	D4	70.0	17.3	Preferred Route, Autumn 1991	--
M4	Junction 12 Improvement, Berkshire	--	1.1	--	Tender Invitation, Winter 1989/90	1990
M4	Widening between Junctions 12 & 15, Berkshire, Wiltshire	D4	77.0	32.0	Preferred Route, 1993	--
M4	Widening between Junctions 18 & 20, Avon	D4	85.0	10.0	Preferred Route, 1992	--
M4	Second Severn Bridge,	D3	--	3.1	Tender Award Early 1990	--
M4/M5	Second Severn Bridge Approach Roads, Avon	D3/D2	69.0	10.0	Route Confirmed Early 1990	--
M5	Junctions 1 & 2 Improvement, Sandwell MB	--	12.0	--	Preferred Route, 1993	--
M5	Widening Warndon -- Strensham (Junctions 6 -- 8), Hereford & Worcester	D3	77.0	13.0	Tender Invitation, Autumn 1990	1991
M5	Junction 12 Improvement, Gloucestershire	--	1.0	--	Preferred Route, 1992	--
M5	Widening between Junctions 15 & 21, Avon	D4	150.0	21.0	Preferred Route, 1992	--
M5	Junction 18 Improvement & Avonmouth Relief Road, Avon	D2	20.0	2.0	Preferred Route, Spring 1990	--
M6	Extension Carlisle -- Guards Mill, Cumbria	D3	50.0	6.0	Preferred Route, Summer 1990	--
M6	Widening between Junctions 30 & 32, Lancashire	D4	56.0	7.0	Orders, Summer 1990	--
M6	Widening between Junctions 20 & 21A, Cheshire	D4	71.0	6.1	Tender Invitation, 1992	--
M6	Widening between Junctions 16 & 20, Cheshire	D4	200.0	23.5	Preferred Route, Autumn 1991	--
M6	Widening between Junctions 11 & 16, Staffordshire	D4	280.0	32.5	Preferred Route, Winter 1991/92	--
M6	Junctions 9 & 10 Improvement, Walsall MB	--	12.0	--	Preferred Route, 1993	--
M6	Widening between M1 & Junction 4 (M42), Warwickshire, Coventry MB, Solihull MB	D4	200.0	24.0	Preferred Route, 1993	--

TABLE 3: NATIONAL TRUNK ROAD PROGRAMME SCHEMES IN PREPARATION AT 1 JANUARY 1990

Route Number	Scheme	Proposed Standard	Estimated Works Cost (£ million November 87 prices)	Approximate Length (Miles)	Next Key Preparation Stage and Target Date *	Start of Works Date
M11	Widening between Junctions 8 & 14, Essex, Cambridgeshire	D3	81.0	25.0	Preferred Route, 1992	--
M11	Junction 5 North Facing Slip Roads, Essex	--	6.6	--	Preferred Route, Autumn 1990	--
M12	M25 -- Chelmsford, Essex	D3/D2	45.0	9.1	Preferred Route, 1993	--
M18	Junction with B6094 Cockhill Lane, Doncaster MB	--	1.9	--	Preferred Route, Autumn 1990	--
M20	Widening between Junctions 3 & 5, Kent	D4	25.0	6.1	Preferred Route, Autumn 1991	--
M20	Widening between Junctions 5 & 8(Maidstone Bypass), Kent	D4/D3	70.0	6.7	Tender Invitation, Summer 1991	--
M23	Widening between Junctions 8 & 9, Surrey	D4	30.0	7.2	Preferred Route, Autumn 1991	--
M25	Widening of Dual 3-Lane Sections, Buckinghamshire, Hertfordshire, Essex, Kent, Surrey	D4	1,000.0	107.0	Subject to M25 Action Plan	--
M40	Widening between Junctions 4 & 5, Buckinghamshire	D3	41.2	7.8	Tender Invitation, Winter 1989/90	1990
M40	Widening between Junctions 1A & 4, Buckinghamshire	D4	70.0	9.6	Preferred Route, 1992	--
M42	Widening between Junction 1 (Lickey End) & Junction 7 (M6), Hereford & Worcester, Warwickshire, Solihull MB	D4	185.0	21.0	Preferred Route, 1993	--
M45/A45	Grade Separated Junction, Dunchurch, Warwickshire	--	1.5	--	Tender Invitation, Spring 1990	1990
M56	Widening between Junctions 4 & 6, Manchester MB, Trafford MB	D4	23.0	2.0	Preferred Route /Orders, Spring 1991	--
M62	M62 East -- M606 Link Road, Kirklees MB	D2	5.0	1.0	Preferred Route, 1992	--
M62	Widening between Junctions 22 & 24, Calderdale MB, Kirklees MB	D4	75.0	9.0	Preferred Route, 1992	--
M62	Widening between Junctions 21 & 22 (Westbound), Rochdale MB	D4	10.0	4.0	Preferred Route /Orders, Winter 1990/91	--
M62	Improvement at Junction 20 (A627(M)), Rochdale MB	--	5.0	--	Orders, Winter 1990/91	--
M62	Widening between Junctions 18 & 21, Rochdale MB	D4	60.0	8.0	Orders, 1993	--
M62	Widening between Junctions 17 & 18, Bury MB	D4	4.0	2.0	Tender Invitation, Winter 1990/91	1991
M62	Widening and Improvement between Junctions 12 & 17, Bury MB, Salford MB	D4	40.0	6.0	Preferred Route, Summer 1990	--

TABLE 3: NATIONAL TRUNK ROAD PROGRAMME SCHEMES IN PREPARATION AT 1 JANUARY 1990

Route Number	Scheme	Proposed Standard	Estimated Works Cost (£ million November 87 prices)	Approximate Length (Miles)	Next Key Preparation Stage and Target Date *	Start of Works Date
M62	Widening between Junctions 6 & 7, Knowsley MB	D4	50.0	3.0	Preferred Route /Orders, 1992	--
M63	Widening between Junctions 7 & 9, Trafford MB, Manchester MB	D4	20.0	3.0	Preferred Route /Orders, Spring 1991	--
M65	Blackburn Southern Bypass, Lancashire	D2	93.0	13.0	Tender Invitation, 1992	--
M66	Denton -- Middleton, Tameside MB, Manchester MB, Oldham MB, Bury MB, Rochdale MB	D4/D3	116.0	11.0	Tender Invitation, Autumn 1991	1992
M606	A6177 Junction Improvement, Bradford MB	--	2.0	--	Preferred Route, Summer 1991	--
M621/M1	Link Road, Leeds MB	D2	7.0	1.0	Preferred Route, Spring 1991	--
A1(M)	Junctions 6 -- 8 and 9--10 Improvements, Hertfordshire	D3	40.0	6.0	Preferred Route, 1992	--
A1(M)	Junctions 1 -- 6 Improvement, Hertfordshire	D4/D3	60.0	13.0	Preferred Route, 1993	--
A6(M)	Stockport North -- South Bypass, Stockport MB	D3/D4 D2	64.0	5.2	Tender Invitation, 1992	1992

ALL PURPOSE TRUNK ROAD SCHEMES

Route Number	Scheme	Proposed Standard	Estimated Works Cost (£ million November 87 prices)	Approximate Length (Miles)	Next Key Preparation Stage and Target Date *	Start of Works Date
A1/M1 Link	Scratchwood Link, LB Barnet	D3	28.2	0.6	Preferred Route, 1993	_
A1	Marshall Meadows Improvement, Northumberland	D2	2.9	1.8	Orders, Spring 1990	--
A1	Brownieside Improvement, Northumberland	D2	2.7	2.1	Orders, Spring 1990	--
A1	Gateshead Western Bypass Improvement, Gateshead MB	D3	13.0	7.0	Preferred Route, Autumn 1991	--
A1	Leeming -- Scotch Corner Improvements, N. Yorkshire	D3	43.0	10.8	Preferred Route, Summer 1991	--
A1	Dishforth -- Leeming Improvements Phase 1 (Gatenby Lane Junction), N. Yorkshire	--	2.5	--	Tender Invitation, Winter 1990/91	1991
A1	Dishforth -- Leeming Improvements Phase 2, N. Yorkshire	D3	54.0	13.8	Preferred Route, Winter 1990/91	--
A1	Wetherby -- Dishforth Improvements, N. Yorkshire	D3	67.1	16.0	Orders, Summer 1990	--
A1	Bramham -- Wetherby Improvements, Leeds MB	D3	19.3	3.8	Tender Invitation, Winter 1989/90	1990
A1	Hook Moor -- Bramham Improvements, Leeds MB, N. Yorkshire	D4	40.0	4.4	Preferred Route, Summer 1990	--

TABLE 3: NATIONAL TRUNK ROAD PROGRAMME SCHEMES IN PREPARATION AT 1 JANUARY 1990

Route Number	Scheme	Proposed Standard	Estimated Works Cost (£ million November 87 prices)	Approximate Length (Miles)	Next Key Preparation Stage and Target Date *	Start of Works Date
A1	Ferrybridge -- Hook Moor Conversion to Motorway, Wakefield MB, Leeds MB, N. Yorkshire	D3	46.0	9.0	Preferred Route, 1992	--
A1	Redhouse -- Ferrybridge Conversion to Motorway, Doncaster MB, Wakefield MB, N. Yorkshire	D3	54.0	9.0	Preferred Route, 1992	--
A1/A57/ A614	Five Lanes End Grade Separated Junction, Nottinghamshire	--	4.0	0.9	Preferred Route, Winter 1989/90	--
A1	Markham Moor Grade Separated Junction, Nottinghamshire	--	4.5	--	Preferred Route, 1993	--
A1	Blyth Grade Separated Junction, Nottinghamshire	--	4.5	--	Preferred Route, 1993	--
A1	Peterborough -- Stamford Improvement, Cambridgeshire	D3	17.0	11.0	Preferred Route, 1993	--
A1	Alconbury -- Peterborough Improvement, Cambridgeshire	D3	31.0	15.0	Preferred Route, Summer 1991	--
A1	Norman Cross Improvements, Cambridgeshire	D3	5.5	1.2	Preferred Route, Autumn 1990	--
A1	Glatton Grade Separated Junction, Cambridgeshire	--	1.5	--	Orders, Winter 1989/90	--
A1	South of Brampton Junction Improvement, Cambridgeshire	D2	1.4	0.8	Tenders Invited, Winter 1989/90	1990
A1	Baldock -- Alconbury Conversion to Motorway Hertfordshire, Bedfordshire, Cambridgeshire	D3	120.0	25.0	Preferred Route, 1993	--
A1	Tempsford Grade Separated Junction, Bedfordshire	--	2.6	--	Tender Invitation, Autumn 1991	--
A1	Langford Turn Grade Separated Junction, Bedfordshire	--	3.0	--	Preferred Route, 1992	--
A2	Kidbrooke Park Road Interchange, LB Greenwich	--	5.8	0.7	Preferred Route, 1993	--
A2/A282	Dartford Improvements, Kent	D4/D2	27.0	6.1	Preferred Route, 1993	--
A2	Lydden (B2060) -- Dover Improvement, Kent	D2	11.5	6.0	Preferred Route, 1993	--
A3	Robin Hood Gate Junction -- Roehampton Vale Improvement, LB Kingston	D3	27.8	1.6	Preferred Route, 1993	--
A3	Hook Interchange Improvement, LB Kingston	D2	10.5	--	Preferred Route, 1993	--
A3	M25 -- A245 Improvement, Surrey	D3	9.0	2.2	Preferred Route, 1993	--
A3	M25 -- B2234 Improvement, Surrey	D3	22.0	5.3	Preferred Route, 1993	--

TABLE 3: NATIONAL TRUNK ROAD PROGRAMME SCHEMES IN PREPARATION AT 1 JANUARY 1990

Route Number	Scheme	Proposed Standard	Estimated Works Cost (£ million November 87 prices)	Approximate Length (Miles)	Next Key Preparation Stage and Target Date *	Start of Works Date
A3	Stoke Road -- Hogs Back (Guildford) Improvement, Surrey	D3	28.2	3.3	Preferred Route, 1993	--
A3	Milford Bypass, Surrey	D2	8.9	1.8	Tender Invitation, Winter 1990/91	--
A3	Hindhead Improvements, Surrey	D2	24.5	4.1	Orders, Spring 1991	--
A3	Liphook & Petersfield Bypasses, Hampshire	D2	47.2	12.6	Tender Invitation, Autumn 1990	--
A4	Waggoners Corner (A312) Junction Improvement, LB Hounslow	--	5.7	--	Preferred Route, 1993	--
A4	Henlys' Corner Junction Improvement, LB Hounslow	--	1.9	--	Preferred Route, 1993	--
A4/A36/ A46	Batheaston / Swainswick Bypass & A36 Link, Avon	D2/S	53.0	3.3	Tender Invitation, 1992	--
A5	Wolfshead -- Weirbrook Improvement, Shropshire	S	1.9	2.5	Preferred Route, 1992	--
A5	Nesscliffe Bypass, Shropshire	D2	6.0	2.9	Preferred Route, Summer 1991	--
A5/A49	Telford -- Shrewsbury Bypass, Shropshire	D2/S	62.8	17.0	Tender Invitation, Winter 1989/90	1990
A5	Weeford -- Fazeley Improvement, Staffordshire	D2	15.0	3.0	Preferred Route, 1993	--
A5	Fazeley, Two Gates & Wilnecote Bypass, Staffordshire	D2	26.7	5.0	Tender Invitation, Spring 1991	--
A5	Kilsby Diversion, Northamptonshire	S	0.9	0.5	Orders, Spring 1990	--
A5	Towcester Bypass, Northamptonshire	S	3.0	2.0	Preferred Route, 1992	--
A5	Little Brickhill -- M1 Buckinghamshire, Bedfordshire, Hertfordshire	D2	33.0	12.2	Preferred Route, 1993	--
A5	Little Brickhill Bypass, Buckinghamshire	D2	6.8	1.6	Tender Invitation, Autumn 1991	--
A5	Sheep Lane Grade Separated Junction, Bedfordshire	--	2.1	--	Orders, Spring 1990	--
A5	Dunstable Bypass, Bedfordshire	D2	30.7	4.6	Preferred Route, Spring 1990	--
A6	Disley & High Lane Bypass Stockport MB, Cheshire, Derbyshire	D2	33.0	4.1	Orders, Summer 1991	--
A6	Kegworth Bypass, Leicestershire	S	3.0	2.0	Preferred Route, Spring 1990	--
A6	Loughborough Bypass, Leicestershire	S	21.0	6.0	Preferred Route, 1992	--

TABLE 3: NATIONAL TRUNK ROAD PROGRAMME SCHEMES IN PREPARATION AT 1 JANUARY 1990

Route Number	Scheme	Proposed Standard	Estimated Works Cost (£ million November 87 prices)	Approximate Length (Miles)	Next Key Preparation Stage and Target Date ✱	Start of Works Date
A6	Quorn & Mountsorrel Bypass, Leicestershire	D2	29.0	4.5	Tenders Invited Autumn, 1989	1990
A6	Great Glen Bypass, Leicestershire	D2/S	5.3	3.1	Orders, Summer 1991	--
A6	Kibworth Bypass, Leicestershire	S	4.0	3.0	Preferred Route, 1992	--
A6	Great Glen -- Market Harborough Improvement, Leicestershire	D2/S	4.5	2.5	Preferred Route, 1992	--
A6	Market Harborough Bypass, Leicestershire	S	7.4	5.4	Tender Invitation, Summer 1990	1990
A6	Market Harbourough -- Desborough Improvement, Northamptonshire	D2/S	6.0	4.0	Preferred Route, 1992	--
A6	Rothwell & Desborough Bypass, Northamptonshire	D2/S	5.5	5.0	Preferred Route, Summer 1990	--
A6	Burton Latimer Bypass, Northamptonshire	S	2.5	2.0	Tender Invitation, Autumn 1990	1990
A6	Finedon Bypass, Northamptonshire	S	2.3	1.3	Preferred Route, 1993	--
A6	Rushden & Higham Ferrers Bypass, Northamptonshire	D2/S	5.1	3.5	Orders, Summer 1990	--
A6	Clapham Bypass, Bedfordshire	D2	10.5	2.4	Orders, Summer 1990	--
A6/A428	Bedford Western Bypass, Bedfordshire	D2	30.0	3.8	Orders, Autumn 1990	--
A10/A47	A134 -- Hardwick Roundabout Improvement, Norfolk	D2	9.6	3.9	Preferred Route, Summer 1991	--
A10	Brandon Creek -- Southery, Norfolk	S	1.0	1.0	Tender Invitation, Spring 1990	1990
A10	Cambridge -- Ely Improvement, Cambridgeshire	D2	22.0	12.0	Preferred Route, 1993	--
A10	Hay Lane -- Buntingford Improvement, Hertfordshire	D2	2.4	1.2	Preferred Route, Spring 1991	--
A10	Wadesmill, High Cross & Colliers End Bypass, Hertfordshire	D2	12.3	4.8	Orders, Summer 1990	--
A10	M25 -- Hoddesdon Improvement, Hertfordshire	D3	15.0	9.1	Preferred Route, 1993	--
A11	Besthorpe -- Wymondham Improvement, Norfolk	D2	15.8	4.9	Tender Invitation, 1992	--
A11	Attleborough Bypass Improvement, Norfolk	D2	6.0	3.0	Preferred Route, 1992	--
A11	Roudham Heath -- Attleborough, Norfolk	D2	17.0	5.4	Preferred Route, Winter 1989/90	--
A11	Fiveways Roundabout -- Bridgham Heath, Norfolk, Suffolk	D2	21.0	12.0	Preferred Route, 1993	--

56

TABLE 3: NATIONAL TRUNK ROAD PROGRAMME SCHEMES IN PREPARATION AT 1 JANUARY 1990

Route Number	Scheme	Proposed Standard	Estimated Works Cost (£ million November 87 prices)	Approximate Length (Miles)	Next Key Preparation Stage and Target Date *	Start of Works Date
A11	Red Lodge Bypass, Suffolk	D2	6.0	1.8	Tender Invitation, Spring 1990	1990
A11	Newmarket -- Red Lodge, Cambridgeshire	D2	4.8	1.4	Orders, Spring 1990	--
A11	Four Wentways -- Newmarket Dualling, Cambridgeshire	D2	10.8	4.7	Orders, Winter 1989/90	--
A11	Four Wentways Junction Improvement, Cambridgeshire	--	9.9	--	Orders, Winter 1989/90	--
A11	Stump Cross -- Four Wentways, Cambridgeshire	D2	9.7	1.6	Orders, Autumn 1990	--
A12	Gorleston Relief Road, Norfolk	D2	15.5	2.6	Tender Invitation, Spring 1991	1991
A12	Lowestoft Second Harbour Crossing, Suffolk	D2	58.0	5.0	Preferred Route, Autumn 1990	--
A12	Saxmundham Bypass -- Lowestoft Widening, Suffolk	D2	27.0	17.0	Preferred Route, 1993	--
A12	Saxmundham Bypass Improvement, Suffolk	D2	6.0	4.0	Preferred Route, 1992	--
A12	Wickham Market -- Saxmundham Bypass, Suffolk	D2	7.8	5.9	Preferred Route, Spring 1991	--
A12	Woodbridge -- Wickham Market Improvement, Suffolk	D2	2.5	1.5	Preferred Route, Winter 1991/92	--
A12	Martlesham -- Woodbridge Improvement, Suffolk	D2	2.0	1.0	Preferred Route, Winter 1991/92	--
A12	Capel St Mary Grade Separated Junction, Suffolk	--	3.9	--	Tenders Invited, Autumn 1989	1990
A12	South of Four Sisters Grade Separated Junction, Suffolk	--	2.0	--	Preferred Route, 1992	--
A12	Hatfield Peverel -- Marks Tey Widening, Essex	D3	15.0	11.0	Preferred Route, 1993	--
A12	Chelmsford Bypass Widening, Essex	D2	14.0	9.8	Preferred Route, 1993	--
A12	Whalebone Lane Junction Improvement, LB Barking & Dagenham	--	4.0	--	Preferred Route, 1993	--
A12	Gallows Corner Intersection Improvement, LB Havering	--	5.5	--	Preferred Route, 1993	--
A12	Hackney Wick -- M11 Link LBs, Hackney, Redbridge, Waltham Forest, Newham	D3/D2	120.0	3.8	Tender Invitation, Winter 1990/91	1991
A13	Wennington -- Mar Dyke, Essex	D3	21.5	3.0	Orders, Winter 1989/90	--
A13	Thames Avenue -- Wennington LBs Barking & Dagenham, Havering	D3	46.6	3.0	Orders, Spring 1990	--
A13	Heathway (A1240) -- Ballards Road Junction Improvement, LB Barking & Dagenham	D2	14.3	--	Preferred Route, Spring 1990	--

57

TABLE 3: NATIONAL TRUNK ROAD PROGRAMME SCHEMES IN PREPARATION AT 1 JANUARY 1990

Route Number	Scheme	Proposed Standard	Estimated Works Cost (£ million November 87 prices)	Approximate Length (Miles)	Next Key Preparation Stage and Target Date *	Start of Works Date
A13	Movers Lane Junction Improvement, LB Barking & Dagenham	D2	17.3	--	Preferred Route, 1993	--
A13	A117 Junction Improvement, LB Newham	D3	18.2	--	Preferred Route, Spring 1990	--
A13	A112 Prince Regent Lane Junction Improvement, LB Newham	D3	25.3	--	Preferred Route, Winter 1990/91	--
A13	Ironbridge Junction Improvement, LB Newham	D3	28.9	--	Orders, Winter 1990/91	--
A13	Leamouth Road Junction Improvement, LB Tower Hamlets	--	1.0	--	Tender Invitation, Winter 1989/90	1990
A13	Cotton Street/Blackwall Tunnel Junction and Tunnel Spur, LB Tower Hamlets	--	35.0	--	Preferred Route, 1993	--
A13	Blackwall Junction Interim Scheme, LB Tower Hamlets	--	1.0	--	Tender Invitation, Summer 1990	1990
A13	West India Dock Road Junction Improvement, LB Tower Hamlets	--	1.0	--	Orders, Winter 1990/91	--
A13	West India Dock Road Interim Junction Improvement, LB Tower Hamlets	--	1.0	--	Tender Invitation, Spring 1990	1990
A13	Butcher Row Junction Improvement, LB Tower Hamlets	--	1.0	--	Orders, Winter 1990/91	--
A14	Bar Hill -- M1 - A1 Link Improvement, Cambridgeshire	D3/D2	45.0	18.0	Preferred Route, 1993	--
A14	M1 - A1 Link, Catthorpe Interchange, Leicestershire	--	3.3	--	Tenders Invited, Autumn 1989	1990
A14	M1 - A1 Link Catthorpe -- Rothwell (A), Northamptonshire	D2	25.4	8.9	Tender Invitation, Winter 1990/91	1991
A14	M1 - A1 Link Catthorpe -- Rothwell (B), Northamptonshire	D2	23.1	8.2	Tender Invitation, Winter 1990/91	1991
A14	M1 - A1 Link Rothwell -- Kettering, Northamptonshire	D2	6.4	1.7	Tenders Invited, Autumn 1989	1990
A14	M1 - A1 Link Kettering Southern Bypass, Northamptonshire	D2	37.2	5.6	Tenders Invited, Autumn 1989	1990
A14	M1 - A1 Link Thrapston -- Brampton (B), Cambridgeshire	D2	7.0	2.9	Tender Invitation, Winter 1990/91	1991
A14	M1 - A1 Link Thrapston -- Brampton (C), Cambridgeshire	D2	13.0	3.0	Tender Invitation, Winter 1990/91	1991
A16	Ludborough Bypass, Lincolnshire	S	1.2	1.5	Orders, Winter 1989/90	--

TABLE 3: NATIONAL TRUNK ROAD PROGRAMME SCHEMES IN PREPARATION AT 1 JANUARY 1990

Route Number	Scheme	Proposed Standard	Estimated Works Cost (£ million November 87 prices)	Approximate Length (Miles)	Next Key Preparation Stage and Target Date *	Start of Works Date
A16	Fotherby Bypass, Lincolnshire	S	1.5	1.5	Preferred Route, Autumn 1990	--
A16	Louth Bypass, Lincolnshire	S	5.5	3.4	Tenders Invited, Autumn 1989	1990
A16	Partney Bypass, Lincolnshire	S	1.1	0.9	Preferred Route, Spring 1991	--
A16	East Keal Bypass, Lincolnshire	S	1.7	1.5	Preferred Route, Summer 1992	--
A16	Stickford Bypass, Lincolnshire	S	1.0	1.0	Orders, Winter 1989/90	--
A16	Boston -- Algarkirk Diversion, Lincolnshire	S	11.7	5.7	Tenders Invited, Autumn 1989	1990
A16	Spalding -- Sutterton Improvement, Lincolnshire	S	22.8	10.9	Tender Invitation, Winter 1991/92	--
A16	Market Deeping/Deeping St James Bypass, Lincolnshire	S	4.8	3.4	Preferred Route, Autumn 1991	--
A16/A43	Stamford Relief Road, Lincolnshire	S	4.1	1.5	Orders, Spring 1991	--
A17	Leadenham Bypass, Lincolnshire	S	2.9	2.8	Tender Invitation, Winter 1991/92	--
A17	Leadenham -- Sleaford Improvement, Lincolnshire	D2/S	6.5	6.0	Preferred Route, Spring 1991	--
A17	Wigtoft -- Sutterton Bypass, Lincolnshire	S	4.4	2.7	Tender Invitation, Spring 1991	--
A17	Sutterton -- Sutton Bridge, Lincolnshire	D2	11.1	15.0	Preferred Route, 1993	--
A17/A47	Tilney High End -- Sutton Bridge, Norfolk	D2	20.0	12.0	Preferred Route, 1993	--
A19	Thormanby Bypass, N. Yorkshire	S	2.0	1.0	Preferred Route, 1992	--
A19	Easingwold Bypass, N. Yorkshire	S	3.8	2.7	Orders, Autumn 1990	--
A19	Shipton by Beningbrough Bypass, N. Yorkshire	S	2.0	1.0	Preferred Route, 1992	--
A19	Norton -- Parkway Interchange, Cleveland	D3	12.0	5.0	Preferred Route, Autumn 1991	--
A20	Folkestone -- Dover Stage 1 (Folkestone -- Court Wood), Kent	D2	31.9	4.5	Tender Invitation, Contract 1, Spring 1990 Contract 2, Winter 1990/91	1990 1991
A20	Folkestone -- Dover Stage 2 (Court Wood -- Dover), Kent	D2	15.0	4.8	Tender Invitation, Winter 1990/91	1991
A21	Tonbridge Bypass -- Pembury Bypass Dualling, Kent	D3	13.6	2.4	Preferred Route , Spring 1990	--
A21	Kipping's Cross -- Lamberhurst Improvement, Kent	D2	9.3	3.0	Preferred Route, Winter 1990/91	--
A21	Lamberhurst Bypass, Kent	D2	5.4	2.0	Orders, Autumn 1991	--
A21	Lamberhurst Bypass -- Chingley Wood Improvement, Kent	D2	5.6	2.1	Preferred Route, 1993	--

TABLE 3: NATIONAL TRUNK ROAD PROGRAMME SCHEMES IN PREPARATION AT 1 JANUARY 1990

Route Number	Scheme	Proposed Standard	Estimated Works Cost (£ million November 87 prices)	Approximate Length (Miles)	Next Key Preparation Stage and Target Date *	Start of Works Date
A21	Flimwell Improvement, Kent, E. Sussex	D2/S	1.8	0.6	Preferred Route, 1993	--
A21	Hurst Green Bypass, E. Sussex	D2	7.0	2.5	Preferred Route, 1993	--
A21	Silver Hill Northbound Climbing Lane, E. Sussex	S	4.0	0.8	Preferred Route, Winter 1990/91	--
A23	Coulsdon Inner Relief Road, LB Croydon	D2	12.1	1.5	Preferred Route, Spring 1990	--
A23	Handcross -- Pease Pottage Improvement, W. Sussex	D3	7.4	2.3	Tender Invitation, 1992	--
A23	Handcross -- Warninglid Improvement, W. Sussex	D3	4.8	2.0	Orders, Winter 1990/91	--
A23	Warninglid -- Brighton (Warninglid Flyover -- Sayers Common), W. Sussex	D3/D2	18.4	4.7	Tender Invitation, Summer 1991	1991
A23	Warninglid -- Brighton (Sayers Common -- Muddleswood), W. Sussex	D2	12.4	2.7	Tenders Invited, Autumn 1989	1990
A23	Warninglid -- Brighton (Muddleswood -- Brighton), W Sussex, E. Sussex	D3/D2	19.5	4.2	Tender Invitation, Spring 1990	1990
A26	Beddingham -- Itford Farm Diversion, E. Sussex	S	3.6	2.0	Preferred Route, Winter 1991/92	--
A27	Polegate Bypass, E. Sussex	D2	13.1	2.8	Preferred Route, Spring 1990	--
A27	Lewes -- Polegate Improvement, E. Sussex	D2	25.1	9.4	Preferred Route, 1993	--
A27	Brighton & Hove Bypass (Patcham -- Coldean), E. Sussex	D2	16.1	2.9	Tender Invitation, Spring 1990	1990
A27	Brighton & Hove Bypass (Hangleton -- Dyke Road), E. Sussex	D2/S	14.0	2.8	Tender Invitation, Spring 1990	1990
A27	Brighton & Hove Bypass (Kingston -- Hangleton), E. Sussex, W. Sussex	D2	22.8	2.4	Tender Invitation, 1992	--
A27	Worthing -- Lancing Improvement, W. Sussex	D3/D2	33.0	6.0	Orders, 1992	--
A27	Patching Junction Improvement, W. Sussex	D2	6.7	1.6	Orders, Summer 1991	--
A27	Crossbush Bypass, W. Sussex	D2	2.8	1.1	Tender Invitation, Summer 1991	--
A27	Arundel Bypass, W. Sussex	D2	15.7	3.4	Orders, Spring 1991	--
A27	Westhampnett Bypass, W. Sussex	D2	8.5	1.9	Tender Invitation, 1992	--
A30/A303	Marsh -- Honiton & Honiton Eastern Bypass, Devon	D2/S	36.0	9.8	Orders, Autumn 1990	--
A30	Honiton -- Exeter Improvement, Devon	D2	38.0	12.0	Orders, Summer 1990	--

TABLE 3: NATIONAL TRUNK ROAD PROGRAMME SCHEMES IN PREPARATION AT 1 JANUARY 1990

Route Number	Scheme	Proposed Standard	Estimated Works Cost (£ million November 87 prices)	Approximate Length (Miles)	Next Key Preparation Stage and Target Date *	Start of Works Date
A30	Woodleigh Grade Separated Junction, Devon	--	1.5	--	Preferred Route, 1993	--
A30	Okehampton -- Launceston Improvement, Devon	D2	35.0	12.8	Tender Invitation, Spring 1991	--
A30	Plusha -- Bolventor Improvement, Cornwall	D2	9.8	5.2	Tender Invitation, Winter 1989/90	1990
A30	Shallowater Hill Improvement, Cornwall	D2	1.6	0.9	Preferred Route, Winter 1989/90	--
A30	Temple -- Higher Carblake Improvement, Cornwall	D2	3.0	3.0	Preferred Route, 1993	--
A30	Bodmin -- Indian Queens Improvement, Cornwall	D2	8.0	7.1	Preferred Route, 1992	--
A30/A39	Indian Queens, Fraddon & St. Columb Road Bypass, Cornwall	D2/S	9.1	5.0	Orders, Winter 1990/91	--
A30	Penhale -- Carland Cross Improvement, Cornwall	D2	8.3	4.6	Tender Invitation, Winter 1989/90	1990
A30	Carland Cross -- Zelah Improvement, Cornwall	S	4.8	2.3	Preferred Route, 1993	--
A30	Zelah Bypass, Cornwall	S	2.6	2.0	Tender Invitation, Spring 1990	1990
A30	Zelah -- Chiverton Improvement, Cornwall	S	5.0	4.0	Preferred Route, 1993	--
A30	St. Erth -- Newtown Improvement, Cornwall	D2	7.0	4.0	Preferred Route, 1993	--
A31	Malwood Hill Improvement, Hampshire	D3	6.0	1.9	Preferred Route, 1993	--
A31	Malwood Hill -- Ringwood Improvements, Hampshire	D3	35.0	10.3	Preferred Route, 1993	--
A31	Stoney Cross Junction Improvement, Hampshire	--	1.5	--	Tender Invitation Summer 1991	--
A31	Picket Post Junction Improvement, Hampshire	--	2.0	--	Tender Invitation, Summer 1990	1990
A31	Ashley Heath Grade Separated Junction, Dorset	D2	3.0	1.0	Orders, Summer 1990	--
A31	Ashley Heath -- Ringwood Improvement, Dorset	D3	2.5	1.0	Preferred Route, Spring 1991	--
A31	Lion Gate -- Roundhouse Improvement, Dorset	D2	1.0	0.8	Orders, Spring 1991	--
A31	Stag Gate Improvement, Dorset	D2	2.0	1.8	Preferred Route, 1993	--
A31	Winterborne Zelston Improvement, Dorset	D2	1.8	1.5	Tender Invitation, 1992	--
A34	Chieveley/M4 (Junction 13) Improvement, Berkshire	D3	13.1	1.2	Preferred Route, Spring 1991	--

61

TABLE 3: NATIONAL TRUNK ROAD PROGRAMME SCHEMES IN PREPARATION AT 1 JANUARY 1990

Route Number	Scheme	Proposed Standard	Estimated Works Cost (£ million November 87 prices)	Approximate Length (Miles)	Next Key Preparation Stage and Target Date *	Start of Works Date
A34	Newbury Bypass, Berkshire, Hampshire	D2	41.7	8.4	Tender Invitation, 1993	--
A35	Tolpuddle -- Puddletown Bypass, Dorset	D2	12.3	5.8	Orders, Winter 1990/91	--
A35	Yellowham Hill -- Troytown Improvement, Dorset	D2	2.7	1.9	Tender Invitation, Autumn 1990	1991
A35	Stinsford -- Cuckoo Lane Improvement, Dorset	D2	1.2	1.2	Orders, Autumn 1990	--
A35	Winterbourne Abbas Bypass, Dorset	S	4.0	3.0	Preferred Route, 1992	--
A35	Chideock -- Morcombelake Bypass, Dorset	S	7.3	3.6	Orders, Autumn 1990	--
A35	Axminster Bypass, Devon	S	8.7	2.9	Tender Invitation, Winter 1989/90	1990
A35	Wilmington Bypass, Devon	S	3.0	2.4	Preferred Route, 1992	--
A36	Beckington -- East of Bath, Avon	D2	46.0	11.0	Preferred Route, 1992	--
A36	Codford -- Heytesbury Improvement, Wiltshire	S	2.3	1.8	Preferred Route, Winter 1989/90	--
A36	Wylye -- Codford Improvement, Wiltshire	D2	2.0	2.0	Preferred Route, 1992	--
A36	Salisbury Bypass, Wiltshire	D2/S	15.0	11.0	Orders, Summer 1991	--
A36	West Wellow Bypass, Hampshire	D2/S	5.0	2.8	Preferred Route, 1992	--
A38	Alrewas -- Barton Turn, (Dogshead Lane), Staffordshire	D2	1.4	2.5	Tender Invitation, Spring 1990	1990
A38	Bell Bridge -- Alrewas, Staffordshire	--	1.1	--	Tender Invitation, Autumn 1991	1991
A38	A5148 Junction Improvement, Staffordshire	--	5.0	--	Preferred Route, 1993	--
A38	Marsh Mills Junction Improvement, Devon	D2	17.5	1.0	Tender Invitation, Winter 1989/90	1990
A38	Saltash -- Trerulefoot Improvement, Cornwall	D2	25.0	8.0	Preferred Route, 1992	--
A38	Liskeard -- Bodmin Improvement, Cornwall	D2	21.0	9.9	Preferred Route, Spring 1991	--
A39	Bucks Cross Improvement, Devon	S	1.0	1.0	Preferred Route, Autumn 1990	--
A39	Clovelly Cross -- Seckington Improvement, Devon	S	1.0	1.5	Orders, Autumn 1990	--
A39	Allins -- South Penlean Improvement, Cornwall	S	1.0	1.0	Preferred Route, Spring 1990	--
A39	Camelford Bypass, Cornwall	S	4.0	2.0	Preferred Route, 1993	--

TABLE 3: NATIONAL TRUNK ROAD PROGRAMME SCHEMES IN PREPARATION AT 1 JANUARY 1990

Route Number	Scheme	Proposed Standard	Estimated Works Cost (£ million November 87 prices)	Approximate Length (Miles)	Next Key Preparation Stage and Target Date *	Start of Works Date
A39	Wadebridge Bypass, Cornwall	S	9.3	2.5	Tender Invitation, Spring 1991	--
A40	Longford -- M50 (Gorsley), Gloucestershire	D2/S	28.0	12.0	Preferred Route, Summer 1990	--
A40	Witney Bypass -- Sturt Farm Improvement, Oxfordshire	D2	1.1	1.1	Tender Invitation, Winter 1991/92	--
A40	Witney Bypass -- Cassington Dualling, Oxfordshire	D2	11.1	5.2	Orders, Autumn 1990	--
A40	North of Oxford Improvement, Oxfordshire	D3/D2	29.0	4.0	Orders, Summer 1991	--
A40	Headington Improvement, Oxfordshire	--	13.0	--	Preferred Route, Autumn 1991	--
A40	B4027 Islip Turn (Wheatley) Improvement, Oxfordshire	--	1.5	--	Tender Invitation, Autumn 1991	--
A40	Long Lane Junction Improvement, LB Hillingdon	--	34.1	--	Tender Invitation, Summer 1990	1990
A40	Gipsy Corner Junction Improvement, LB Hounslow	--	25.3	--	Tender Invitation, Winter 1991/92	_
A40	Western Circus Junction Improvement, LB Ealing	--	30.4	--	Tender Invitation, Winter 1991/92	_
A40	Long Lane -- West End Road, LB Hillingdon	D3	2.1	1.9	Preferred Route, 1993	--
A41	Milton Green Bypass, Cheshire	S	1.6	1.0	Preferred Route, Winter 1990/91	--
A41	No Mans Heath & Macefen Bypass, Cheshire	S	2.0	1.5	Preferred Route, Summer 1991	--
A41	Whitchurch Bypass, Shropshire	S	7.4	3.4	Tender Invitation, Winter 1989/90	1990
A41	Weston Heath Improvement, Shropshire	S	1.6	2.1	Preferred Route, 1993	--
A41/A421	Bicester Bypass Stage 2 (A421 Bicester -- Wendlebury (M40)), Oxfordshire	D2	4.0	1.9	Tender Invitation, Summer 1991	1991
A41	Aston Clinton Bypass, Buckinghamshire	D2	12.8	3.4	Tender Invitation, Autumn 1991	--
A41	Berkhamsted Bypass, Hertfordshire	D2	26.1	7.2	Tender Invitation, Summer 1991	--
A41	Kings Langley Bypass, Hertfordshire	D2	23.3	4.6	Tender Invitation, Summer 1991	--
A42	Castle Donington North Contracts 2 and 3, Leicestershire	D2	18.4	4.3	Contract 2 Tenders Invited, Autumn 1989 Contract 3 Tender Invitation, Spring 1990	1990
A43	Geddington Bypass, Northamptonshire	D2	10.0	4.3	Preferred Route, Spring 1991	--
A43	Kettering Northern Bypass (M1 - A1 Link), Northamptonshire	D2/S	5.6	2.8	Tender Invitation, Winter 1990/91	1991

63

TABLE 3: NATIONAL TRUNK ROAD PROGRAMME SCHEMES IN PREPARATION AT 1 JANUARY 1990

Route Number	Scheme	Proposed Standard	Estimated Works Cost (£ million November 87 prices)	Approximate Length (Miles)	Next Key Preparation Stage and Target Date *	Start of Works Date
A43	Kettering Northern Bypass (M1 - A1 Link) Advanced Bridge Works, Northamptonshire	--	3.4	--	Tender Invitation, Winter 1989/90	1990
A43	Moulton -- Broughton Dualling, Northamptonshire	D2	8.8	5.7	Preferred Route, Winter 1990/91	--
A43	Moulton Bypass, Northamptonshire	D2	3.4	0.8	Preferred Route, Winter 1990/91	--
A43	Blisworth & Milton Malsor Bypass, Northamptonshire	D2	13.7	4.5	Tender Invitation, Winter 1989/90	1990
A43	Silverstone Bypass, Northamptonshire	D2	11.0	4.7	Orders, Spring 1991	--
A43	Whitfield Turn -- Brackley Hatch Dualling, Northamptonshire	D2	4.9	2.7	Orders Summer, 1991	--
A43	M40 -- B4031 Dualling, Oxfordshire, Northamptonshire	D2	7.7	3.7	Preferred Route, Summer 1991	--
A45	Quarries Cross Improvements, Suffolk	D2	2.2	--	Preferred Route, 1992	--
A45	Rookery Cross Road Grade Separated Junction, Suffolk	--	1.3	--	Preferred Route, 1992	--
A45	M11 -- A10 Improvement, Cambridgeshire	D3	7.5	3.0	Preferred Route, 1992	--
A45	Eaton Socon(A1) -- Hardwick Improvement, Cambridgeshire	D2	36.0	15.0	Preferred Route, 1993	--
A45	Weedon, Flore & Upper Heyford Bypass, Northamptonshire	D2/S	8.0	4.0	Preferred Route, Spring 1991	--
A45 /A452	Stonebridge Grade Separated Junction, Warwickshire, Solihull MB	--	4.0	--	Preferred Route, Spring 1990	--
A45	Broad Lane, Tile Hill Lane Junction Improvement, Coventry MB	--	10.0	--	Preferred Route, 1993	--
A45	Leamington Road Junction Improvement, Coventry MB	--	5.0	--	Preferred Route, 1993	--
A45	Sir Henry Parkes Road, Kenilworth Road Junction Improvement, Coventry MB	--	15.0	--	Preferred Route, 1993	--
A45	A445 Junction Improvement, Warwickshire	--	1.1	--	Orders, Spring 1991	--
A46	Newark (A1133) -- Lincoln Improvement, Nottinghamshire, Lincolnshire	D2	12.0	8.0	Preferred Route, Spring 1991	--
A46	Newark -- Widmerpool Improvement, Nottinghamshire	D2/S	20.0	17.0	Preferred Route, Summer 1991	--
A46	Leicester Western Bypass, Leicestershire	D2	52.4	7.6	Tender Invitation, Winter 1991/92	--

TABLE 3: NATIONAL TRUNK ROAD PROGRAMME SCHEMES IN PREPARATION AT 1 JANUARY 1990

Route Number	Scheme	Proposed Standard	Estimated Works Cost (£ million November 87 prices)	Approximate Length (Miles)	Next Key Preparation Stage and Target Date *	Start of Works Date
A46	Pennsylvania -- Tormarton Improvement, Avon	D2	9.0	2.5	Preferred Route, Winter 1989/90	
A46	Upper Swainswick -- Pennsylvania, Avon	D2	12.0	3.5	Preferred Route , Winter 1989/90	--
A47	Acle Straight Improvement, Norfolk	D2	7.0	7.0	Preferred Route, 1992	--
A47	Blofield -- Acle, Norfolk	D2	3.4	2.1	Preferred Route, Winter 1990/91	--
A47	Norwich Southern Bypass, Norfolk	D2	68.2	14.0	Tender Invitation, Winter 1989/90	1990
A47	East Dereham -- North Tuddenham Improvements, Norfolk	D2	8.9	3.1	Tender Invitation, Summer 1991	--
A47	Hardwick Roundabout -- Easton, Norfolk	D2	58.0	27.0	Preferred Route, 1993	--
A47	Narborough Bypass, Norfolk	S	2.8	1.4	Tender Invitation, Spring 1991	--
A47	Walpole Highway/Tilney High End Bypass, Norfolk	D2	12.6	5.6	Orders, Spring 1990	--
A47	Thorney -- East of Wisbech Improvement, Cambridgeshire	D2	32.5	21.0	Preferred Route, 1993	--
A47	Thorney Bypass, Cambridgeshire	D2	5.0	2.0	Orders, Winter 1990/91	--
A47	Peterborough -- Thorney Improvement, Cambridgeshire	D2	14.5	7.0	Preferred Route, 1992	--
A47	Eye Bypass, Cambridgeshire	S	7.9	3.3	Tenders Invited, Autumn 1989	1990
A47	Castor -- Ailsworth Bypass, Cambridgeshire	D2/S	9.7	3.3	Tenders Invited, Autumn 1989	1990
A47	Sutton -- West of A1, Cambridgeshire	D2	4.7	2.9	Preferred Route, Spring 1991	--
A47	East Norton Bypass, Leicestershire	S	1.4	1.1	Tender Invitation, Winter 1989/90	1990
A49	Improvement between Weaverham and Lower Whitley, Cheshire	S	9.0	1.5	Preferred Route, Winter 1991/92	--
A49	Weaverham Diversion, Cheshire	S	5.0	3.5	Tender Invitation, Summer 1990	1990
A49	Tiverton Bypass, Cheshire	S	3.0	1.5	Preferred Route, Winter 1991/92	--
A49	Preston Brockhurst Bypass, Shropshire	S	1.5	1.3	Preferred Route, Winter 1991/92	--
A49	Dorrington Bypass, Shropshire	D2/S	10.0	4.5	Orders, Summer 1990	--
A49	Stretford Bridge -- Upper Affcot, Shropshire	S	1.2	1.0	Orders, Spring 1990	--
A49	Woofferton Skew Bridge Improvement, Shropshire	S	1.9	1.0	Orders, Spring 1990	--

TABLE 3: NATIONAL TRUNK ROAD PROGRAMME SCHEMES IN PREPARATION AT 1 JANUARY 1990

Route Number	Scheme	Proposed Standard	Estimated Works Cost (£ million November 87 prices)	Approximate Length (Miles)	Next Key Preparation Stage and Target Date *	Start of Works Date
A49	Craven Arms Bypass, Shropshire	S	2.8	1.9	Preferred Route, 1993	--
A49	Onibury -- Stokesay, Shropshire	S	1.3	1.9	Tender Invitation, Winter 1991/92	1992
A49	Ashton Bypass, Hereford & Worcester	S	3.0	2.0	Preferred Route, 1992	--
A49/A465	Hereford Bypass, Hereford & Worcester	D2/S	19.0	9.0	Orders, Spring 1990	--
A50	Blythe Bridge -- Queensway, Staffordshire	D3/D2	80.0	5.0	Orders, Winter 1989/90	--
A51	Improvement between A41 and A54, Cheshire	D2	9.0	3.0	Preferred Route, 1992	--
A51	Duddon and Clotton Bypass, Cheshire	S	3.0	2.0	Preferred Route, Winter 1991/92	--
A51	Tarporley Bypass -- Four Lane Ends, Cheshire	S	1.0	0.5	Preferred Route, Winter 1991/92	--
A51	Alpraham -- Calveley Bypass, Cheshire	S	3.0	1.5	Preferred Route, Winter 1991/92	--
A51	Improvement at Burford and the Green Bypass, Cheshire	S	2.0	2.0	Preferred Route, Summer 1991	--
A52	Ashbourne Relief Road, Derbyshire	S	2.5	1.6	Orders, Winter 1990/91	--
A52	Radcliffe-on-Trent -- Grantham (A1) Improvement, Nottinghamshire, Leicestershire, Lincolnshire	D2	20.0	16.0	Preferred Route, 1993	--
A54	Kelsall Bypass to A556, Cheshire	D2	2.0	0.5	Preferred Route, Winter 1991/92	--
A56	Improvement at A682 Junction (Haslingden Bypass), Lancashire	--	5.0	--	Preferred Route /Orders, 1992	--
A57/A628	Mottram/Hollingworth/ Tintwistle Bypass, Tameside MB, Derbyshire	D2	30.0	4.0	Preferred Route, 1992	--
A58	Wigan, Hindley & Westhoughton Bypass, Bolton MB, Wigan MB	D3/D2	61.0	10.0	Preferred Route, Spring 1990	--
A59	East & West Marton Bypass, N. Yorkshire	S	6.0	4.0	Preferred Route, 1993	--
A59	Improvements East of Gisburn, Lancashire	S	6.0	4.0	Tender Invitation, Summer 1990	--
A59	Copster Green Bypass, Lancashire	S	4.0	2.5	Preferred Route, Winter 1990/91	--
A59	Mellor Brook Bypass, Lancashire	S	2.0	1.0	Tender Invitation, Winter 1990/91	--
A59	Ormskirk -- Walmer Bridge Improvement, Lancashire	D2	30.0	11.0	Preferred Route, 1992	--

TABLE 3: NATIONAL TRUNK ROAD PROGRAMME SCHEMES IN PREPARATION AT 1 JANUARY 1990

Route Number	Scheme	Proposed Standard	Estimated Works Cost (£ million November 87 prices)	Approximate Length (Miles)	Next Key Preparation Stage and Target Date *	Start of Works Date
A63	Castle Street Improvement, Hull, Humberside	D3	8.0	1.0	Preferred Route, 1992	--
A63	Melton Grade Separated Junction, Humberside	--	3.5	--	Preferred Route, Spring 1990	--
A63	Selby Bypass, N. Yorkshire	S	21.0	6.1	Tender Invitation, 1993	--
A63	West of A1 Junction, Leeds MB	D2	30.0	4.0	Preferred Route, 1992	--
A64	Staxton Diversion, N. Yorkshire	S	4.4	2.8	Preferred Route, Autumn 1990	--
A64	Rillington Bypass, N. Yorkshire	D2	6.7	4.4	Preferred Route, Summer 1990	--
A64	York Bypass -- Malton Bypass Dualling, N. Yorkshire	D2	16.0	12.0	Preferred Route, Autumn 1991	--
A65	Burley-in-Wharfedale Bypass, Bradford MB	D2	6.7	1.7	Orders, Autumn 1990	--
A65	Hornsbarrow Diversion, Cumbria	S	2.0	1.0	Preferred Route, Autumn 1990	--
A65	Moss Side -- Lupton, Cumbria	S	1.2	1.1	Preferred Route, Autumn 1991	--
A65	Hellifield & Long Preston Bypass, N. Yorkshire	S	8.8	4.4	Orders, Winter 1990/91	--
A65	Coniston Cold Bypass, N. Yorkshire	S	3.0	1.0	Preferred Route, 1992	--
A65	Gargrave Bypass, N. Yorkshire	S	7.4	3.7	Tender Invitation, Autumn 1991	--
A65	Draughton Bypass, N. Yorkshire	S	3.6	1.5	Tender Invitation, Summer 1990	1990
A65	Ilkley Bypass, Bradford MB	S	13.0	3.0	Preferred Route, Autumn 1991	--
A65	Manor Park Improvement, Bradford MB	D2	5.6	1.6	Preferred Route, Autumn 1990	--
A66	Stainburn & Great Clifton Bypass, Cumbria	S	3.5	2.5	Orders, Autumn 1990	--
A66	Stainmore -- Banksgate Improvement, Cumbria	D2	6.0	3.7	Orders, Autumn 1990	--
A66	Temple Sowerby Bypass and Improvement to Winderwath, Cumbria	S	3.8	2.3	Preferred Route, Autumn 1991	--
A66	Bowes Bypass to County Boundary Improvement, Durham	D2	6.8	6.0	Tender Invitation, Autumn 1990	1990
A66	Longnewton Grade Separated Junction, Cleveland	--	2.4	--	Orders, 1992	--
A69	Haltwhistle Relief Road, Northumberland	S	4.7	1.3	Preferred Route, Winter 1990/91	--
A102	Blackwall Tunnel Third Bore, LBs Tower Hamlets, Greenwich	S	80.0	1.0	Preferred Route, 1993	--
A127	M25 -- Rayleigh, Essex	D4/D2	60.0	12.0	Preferred Route, 1992	--

TABLE 3: NATIONAL TRUNK ROAD PROGRAMME SCHEMES IN PREPARATION AT 1 JANUARY 1990

Route Number	Scheme	Proposed Standard	Estimated Works Cost (£ million November 87 prices)	Approximate Length (Miles)	Next Key Preparation Stage and Target Date *	Start of Works Date
A140	Scole -- Norwich Improvement, Norfolk	D2	26.0	16.0	Preferred Route, 1993	--
A140	Dickleburgh Bypass, Norfolk	S	2.4	1.9	Tenders Invited, Autumn 1989	1990
A140	Scole Bypass, Norfolk	D2/S	3.0	1.3	Orders, Summer 1990	--
A140	Beacon Hill (A45) -- Scole Improvement, Suffolk	D2	38.0	15.5	Preferred Route,1993	--
A167	Durham Western Bypass, Durham	D2	10.1	3.8	Orders, Spring 1990	--
A167	Cock o' the North -- Aycliffe Improvement, Durham	D2	13.0	10.0	Preferred Route, 1992	--
A205	Catford Town Centre Improvements, LB Lewisham	D2	5.8	0.6	Tender Invitation, Spring 1990	--
A249	Brielle Way (Sheerness) Improvement, Kent	S	0.5	0.1	Orders, Autumn 1990	--
A249	Iwade Bypass -- Queenborough, including new Swale Crossing, Kent	D2	36.5	2.5	Preferred Route, 1993	--
A249	Iwade Bypass, Kent	D2	13.0	3.4	Orders, Spring 1990	--
A249	A2 -- M2 Dualling, Kent	D2	13.5	3.1	Orders, Autumn 1990	--
A259	Dymchurch -- M20 (Junction 11), Kent	S	9.0	3.5	Preferred Route, Spring 1990	--
A259	St Mary's Bay & Dymchurch Bypass, Kent	S	10.7	5.2	Preferred Route, Spring 1990	--
A259	New Romney Bypass, Kent	S	4.0	2.2	Preferred Route, Spring 1990	--
A259	Brookland Diversion, Kent	S	1.0	0.7	Orders, Summer 1991	--
A259	Walland Marsh Improvement, Kent	S	4.0	2.2	Preferred Route, 1993	--
A259	Icklesham Diversion, E. Sussex	S	2.0	1.4	Preferred Route, Autumn 1991	--
A259	Guestling Thorn Diversion, E. Sussex	S	1.2	1.1	Tender Invitation, Spring 1991	--
A259	Hastings Eastern Bypass, E. Sussex	S	8.3	3.6	Preferred Route, Summer 1991	--
A259	Bexhill & Hastings Western Bypass, E. Sussex	D2	29.7	8.9	Preferred Route, Autumn 1990	--
A259	Pevensey -- Bexhill Improvement, E. Sussex	D2	4.5	2.2	Preferred Route, 1993	--
A282	Dartford -- Thurrock Crossing Approach Roads, Essex	D4	4.4	0.6	Tender Invitation, Winter 1989/90	1990
A303	Bullington Cross -- Andover Improvements, Hampshire	--	2.5	--	Orders, Autumn 1991	--
A303	Amesbury -- Berwick Down Improvement, Wiltshire	D2	6.0	5.0	Preferred Route, 1992	--

TABLE 3: NATIONAL TRUNK ROAD PROGRAMME SCHEMES IN PREPARATION AT 1 JANUARY 1990

Route Number	Scheme	Proposed Standard	Estimated Works Cost (£ million November 87 prices)	Approximate Length (Miles)	Next Key Preparation Stage and Target Date *	Start of Works Date
A303	Wylye -- Stockton Wood, Wiltshire	D2	2.5	2.5	Preferred Route, 1992	--
A303	Stockton Wood -- Chicklade Bottom, Wiltshire	D2	1.0	1.0	Tender Invitation, Spring 1990	1990
A303	Chicklade Bottom -- Mere, Wiltshire	D2	6.0	6.0	Preferred Route, 1992	--
A303	Mere -- Wincanton Improvement, Somerset	D2	9.7	4.8	Tender Invitation, Spring 1990	1990
A303	Sparkford -- Ilchester Improvement, Somerset	D2	4.6	2.9	Preferred Route, 1992	--
A303	Ilminster -- Marsh, Somerset	D2	5.5	3.9	Preferred Route, 1991	--
A339	Black Dam Grade Separated Junction (Basingstoke), Hampshire	--	5.0	--	Preferred Route, 1993	--
A339	Basingstoke Northern Bypass Stage 3 Dualling, Hampshire	D2	4.7	2.5	Tender Invitation, Spring 1991	--
A339	Basingstoke -- Headley Bypass Improvements, Hampshire	D2	23.0	7.2	Preferred Route, 1993	--
A339	Headley Bypass, Hampshire	D2	9.1	3.3	Preferred Route, Winter 1991/92	--
A339	Headley Bypass -- Newbury Improvements, Hampshire, Berkshire	D2	6.1	1.9	Preferred Route, 1993	--
A380	A38 -- Torbay Trunking & Improvement, Kingskerswell Bypass, Devon	D2	26.0	3.5	Orders, Spring 1991	--
A406	East London River Crossing, LBs Greenwich, Newham	D3/D2	196.7	5.7	Orders, Winter 1989/90	--
A406	Dysons Road -- Hall Lane, LB Enfield	D3/D2	65.5	1.5	Tender Invitation, Winter 1991/92	--
A406	East of Silver Street -- A1010, LB Enfield	D3/D2	40.2	0.7	Tender Invitation, Winter 1991/92	--
A406	Bounds Green -- Green Lanes Improvement, LB Enfield	D2	74.7	2.2	Tender Invitation, 1993	--
A406	Falloden Way -- Finchley High Road, LB Barnet	D3/D2	35.1	1.9	Tender Invitation, Autumn 1991	--
A406	Regents Park Road Junction Improvement, LB Barnet	D3/D2	40.0	--	Tender Invitation, Summer 1991	--
A406	Golders Green Road Junction Improvement, LB Barnet	D3/D2	14.3	--	Orders, Autumn 1990	--
A406	Hanger Lane -- Harrow Road, LB Brent, LB Ealing	D3/D2	85.5	1.7	Tender Invitation, Summer 1990	1990
A406	Popes Lane -- Western Ave, LB Ealing, LB Hounslow	D3/D2	54.0	2.3	Orders, Spring 1990	--

TABLE 3: NATIONAL TRUNK ROAD PROGRAMME SCHEMES IN PREPARATION AT 1 JANUARY 1990

Route Number	Scheme	Proposed Standard	Estimated Works Cost (£ million November 87 prices)	Approximate Length (Miles)	Next Key Preparation Stage and Target Date *	Start of Works Date
A406	Ironbridge -- Neasden Improvement, LB Brent	D3	2.5	0.2	Preferred Route, 1993	--
A417	M5 -- A40 Elmbridge Court, Gloucestershire	D2	14.0	2.0	Preferred Route, 1992	--
A417	Brockworth Bypass, Gloucestershire	D2	43.0	3.2	Orders, Autumn 1990	--
A417	Crickley Hill Improvement, Gloucestershire	D2	1.8	0.9	Preferred Route, Autumn 1990	--
A417	Birdlip -- Crickley Hill, Gloucestershire	D2	3.7	1.7	Preferred Route, 1993	--
A417	Stratton -- Birdlip Dualling, Gloucestershire	D2	9.3	8.1	Orders, Summer 1990	--
A417/A419	Cirencester & Stratton Bypass, Gloucestershire	D2	16.0	7.0	Preferred Route, Winter 1989/90	--
A419	Latton Bypass, Wiltshire	D2	6.0	2.3	Orders, Winter 1990/91	--
A419	Blunsdon Bypass, Wiltshire	D2	5.0	1.0	Preferred Route, 1992	--
A420	Cumnor Hill -- Tubney Manor Improvement, Oxfordshire	D2	6.0	1.9	Preferred Route, 1993	--
A420	Tubney Wood -- Kingston Bagpuize Bypass Improvement, Oxfordshire	D2	6.0	1.9	Preferred Route, 1993	--
A420	Kingston Bagpuize & Southmoor Bypass, Oxfordshire	D2	5.3	2.8	Tender Invitation, Winter 1991/92	--
A420	Southmoor Bypass -- Shrivenham Bypass Improvements, Oxfordshire	D2	40.0	14.4	Preferred Route, 1993	--
A422	Alcester -- Stratford Improvement, Warwickshire	D2	4.0	3.5	Preferred Route, Winter 1990/91	--
A423	Southam Bypass, Warwickshire	S	2.3	1.6	Tender Invitation, Winter 1990/91	--
A423	Maidenhead Thicket -- Burchetts Green, Berkshire	D2	15.5	2.2	Tender Invitation, Summer 1990	1990
A428	Great Barford Bypass and Extension to A1, Bedfordshire	D2	22.5	4.8	Preferred Route, Autumn 1990	--
A428	Bedford Southern Bypass, Bedfordshire	D2	51.9	5.4	Tender Invitation, 1992	--
A428	Lavendon Bypass, Buckinghamshire	S	2.5	1.6	Orders, Autumn 1990	--
A435	Studley Bypass, Warwickshire, Hereford & Worcester	D2	22.9	7.1	Tender Invitation, 1992	--
A435	Norton Lenchwick Bypass, Warwickshire, Hereford & Worcester	D2	21.0	7.6	Tender Invitation, 1992	--

TABLE 3: NATIONAL TRUNK ROAD PROGRAMME SCHEMES IN PREPARATION AT 1 JANUARY 1990

Route Number	Scheme	Proposed Standard	Estimated Works Cost (£ million November 87 prices)	Approximate Length (Miles)	Next Key Preparation Stage and Target Date *	Start of Works Date
A435/A438	South of Evesham -- M5 Improvement, Gloucestershire, Hereford & Worcester	D2	25.0	10.0	Preferred Route, 1993	--
A453	Clifton Lane Improvement, Nottinghamshire	D2	21.0	3.5	Preferred Route, Summer 1990	--
A453	M1 -- Clifton Improvement, Nottinghamshire	D2	11.0	4.0	Preferred Route, Summer 1990	--
A465	Llangua -- Pontrilas, Hereford & Worcester	S	3.0	1.0	Preferred Route, 1992	--
A483	Pant / Llanymynech Bypass, Shropshire	S	5.5	4.3	Preferred Route, Spring 1991	--
A500	Basford -- Hough -- Shavington Bypass, Cheshire	D2/S	12.0	5.0	Preferred Route, Spring 1990	--
A500	City Road & Stoke Road Junction Improvement, Staffordshire	D3/D2	16.0	1.0	Preferred Route, 1993	--
A516	North of Etwall Improvement, Derbyshire	D2/S	2.0	1.0	Preferred Route, 1994	--
A516	Etwall Bypass, Derbyshire	S	3.1	1.5	Tender Invitation, Autumn 1990	--
A523	Poynton Bypass, Cheshire	D2	13.5	3.9	Preferred Route, Summer 1990	--
A523	Improvements, Poynton to Macclesfield, Cheshire	S	5.0	3.0	Preferred Route, 1992	--
A523	Macclesfield Relief Road, Cheshire	D2/S	23.0	5.2	Tender Invitation, Winter 1989/90	1990
A523	Packsaddle -- Rushton Spencer Improvement, Staffordshire	S	4.6	2.8	Preferred Route, 1993	--
A523	Leek Bypass, Staffordshire	S	8.0	5.0	Preferred Route, 1993	--
A523	Miles Knoll -- Waterhouses Improvement, Staffordshire	S	1.2	0.9	Preferred Route, 1993	--
A550	Ledsham to M53 Improvement, Cheshire	D2	3.0	2.0	Preferred Route, Winter 1990/91	--
A550	A5177 Woodbank Junction -- Ledsham, Cheshire	D2	11.0	3.0	Preferred Route, Spring 1990	--
A556	Improvement between M6 & A559, Cheshire	D2	9.0	3.0	Preferred Route, 1992	--
A556	Delamere to Oakmere/ Norley Lane -- A49, Cheshire	S	5.0	5.5	Preferred Route, 1992	--
A564	Doveridge Bypass, Derbyshire	D2	14.6	4.8	Orders, 1992	--
A564	Foston -- Hatton -- Hilton Bypass, Derbyshire	D2	25.0	5.8	Orders, Winter 1989/90	--
A564	Derby Southern Bypass & Derby Spur, Derbyshire	D3/D2	82.5	19.3	Orders, Winter 1989/90	--

TABLE 3: NATIONAL TRUNK ROAD PROGRAMME SCHEMES IN PREPARATION AT 1 JANUARY 1990

Route Number	Scheme	Proposed Standard	Estimated Works Cost (£ million November 87 prices)	Approximate Length (Miles)	Next Key Preparation Stage and Target Date *	Start of Works Date
A568	Widnes Eastern Bypass (North), Cheshire	D2	14.5	3.2	Tender Invitation, Summer 1991	--
A568	Widnes Eastern Bypass (South), Cheshire	S	4.5	1.6	Orders, Autumn 1990	--
A570	Scarisbrick & Pinfold Bypass, Lancashire	D2	10.0	3.0	Preferred Route, 1992	--
A570	Ormskirk Bypass, Lancashire	S	16.0	6.0	Preferred Route, 1992	--
A580	Corridor Improvements (Liverpool -- Manchester), Knowsley MB, St. Helens MB, Wigan MB, Salford MB	D2	15.0	19.0	Tender Invitation , Summer 1990	--
A585	Fleetwood Dock Street Diversion, Lancashire	S	2.5	1.4	Orders, Winter 1989/90	--
A585	Norcross -- M55 Link, Lancashire	D2	32.0	7.5	Preferred Route, Summer 1990	--
A590	High and Low Newton Bypass, Cumbria	D2	6.0	2.5	Orders, Summer 1991	--
A590	Bouth Toll Bar -- Greenodd, Cumbria	S	1.0	1.0	Orders, Autumn 1990	--
A590	Ulverston -- Dalton Bypass, Cumbria	D2	6.0	2.0	Preferred Route, Spring 1991	--
A590	Dalton-in-Furness Bypass, Cumbria	S	9.0	2.1	Tender Invitation, Spring 1991	--
A595	Duddon Bridge Improvement, Cumbria	S	2.0	0.6	Preferred Route, 1992	--
A595	Parton -- Lillyhall Improvement, Cumbria	S	9.0	3.0	Preferred Route, 1992	--
A595	Hensingham Bypass, Cumbria	S	4.0	1.0	Tender Invitation, Spring 1990	1990
A595	Egremont Bypass, Cumbria	S	7.5	2.9	Tender Invitation, Summer 1990	1990
A596	Carlisle Southern Bypass, Cumbria	S	6.0	4.0	Preferred Route, 1992	--
A596	Wigton Bypass, Cumbria	S	4.0	2.7	Tender Invitation, Summer 1990	1990
A616/A628	Salters Brook -- Stocksbridge Improvement, Barnsley MB, Sheffield MB	S	11.0	6.9	Preferred Route, 1992	--
A628	Tintwhistle -- Salters Brook Improvement, Derbyshire	S	3.5	8.0	Preferred Route, 1992	--
A629	Skipton -- Kildwick Improvement, N. Yorkshire	D2	6.6	2.5	Tender Invitation, Summer 1991	--
A638	Doncaster North Bridge Relief Road, Doncaster MB	D2	8.2	1.1	Tender Invitation, Autumn 1991	--
A650	Hard Ings Road Improvement, Bradford MB	D2	5.0	1.0	Preferred Route, 1992	--

TABLE 3: NATIONAL TRUNK ROAD PROGRAMME SCHEMES IN PREPARATION AT 1 JANUARY 1990

Route Number	Scheme	Proposed Standard	Estimated Works Cost (£ million November 87 prices)	Approximate Length (Miles)	Next Key Preparation Stage and Target Date *	Start of Works Date
A650	Airedale Route (Crossflatts -- Cottingley Bar), Bradford MB	D2	31.2	3.0	Tender Invitation, 1993	--
A650	Airedale Route (Crossflatts -- Cottingley Bar, Advanced Bridge Works), Bradford MB	--	2.6	--	Tender Invitation, Winter 1991/92	--
A650	Drighlington Bypass, Leeds MB	S	8.1	2.7	Tender Invitation, Winter 1989/90	1990
A650	Shipley Eastern Bypass, Bradford MB	D2	24.1	2.4	In Abeyance	
A1033	Hedon Road Improvement (Stage 1), Humberside	D2	6.4	1.2	Preferred Route, Spring 1990	--
A1033	Hedon Road Improvement (Stage 2), Humberside	D2	9.0	2.0	Preferred Route, Autumn 1990	--
A1079	Shiptonthorpe Bypass, Humberside	S	1.0	1.0	Preferred Route, 1993	--
A1079	Market Weighton Bypass, Humberside	S	3.1	2.8	Tender Invitation, Winter 1989/90	1990
A1237	York Northern Bypass Dualling, N. Yorkshire	D2	8.0	8.0	Preferred Route, Autumn 1990	--
A6120	Leeds Outer Ring Road Improvement, Leeds MB	D2	12.0	1.2	Preferred Route, Spring 1991	--
A6120	Seacroft & Crossgates Bypass, Leeds MB	D2	12.0	5.0	Preferred Route, 1992	--
	M56 -- A6(M) Link, Cheshire, Stockport MB, Manchester MB	D2	40.0	8.0	Orders, Summer 1990	--
	Preston Southern & Western Bypass, Lancashire	D2/D3	80.0	10.0	Preferred Route, Winter 1991/92	--
	M1 - M62 Link Road (Wakefield -- Kirklees), Wakefield MB, Kirklees MB, Calderdale MB	D2	54.0	12.0	Preferred Route, 1992	--
	Western Environmental Improvement Route, LBs Hammersmith & Fulham, Kensington & Chelsea	D2	97.5	2.4	Preferred Route, Spring 1990	--
	Exeter Northern Bypass, Devon	D2	53.0	7.0	Preferred Route, 1992	--
	Leicester Eastern Bypass (A6 -- A46), Leicestershire	D2/S	45.0	8.0	Preferred Route, 1994	--

TABLE 3: NATIONAL TRUNK ROAD PROGRAMME SCHEMES IN PREPARATION AT 1 JANUARY 1990

Route Number	Scheme	Proposed Standard	Estimated Works Cost (£ million November 87 prices)	Approximate Length (Miles)	Next Key Preparation Stage and Target Date *	Start of Works Date
A31 -- Poole Harbour Trunking & Improvements						
	A31 -- Mannings Heath Relief Road, Dorset	D2	23.0	5.5	Preferred Route, 1992	--
	Poole Harbour Bridge Replacement, Dorset	D2	17.0	0.9	Preferred Route, 1993	--
East - West Route West of Aylesbury -- A12						
	West of Aylesbury -- Wing Bypass, Buckinghamshire	D2	35.0	14.0	Preferred Route, Spring 1991	--
	A5 -- A1, Hertfordshire, Bedfordshire	D2/D3	40.0	13.8	Preferred Route, 1992	--
	A1 -- Stansted, Hertfordshire, Essex	D2/D3	65.0	18.3	Preferred Route, 1992	--
	Braintree -- A12, Essex	D2	25.0	7.5	Preferred Route, 1992	--

NOTES

* For explanation of scheme preparation stages and timings see paragraphs 3.15 -- 3.17 and Annex A.

S   = Single carriageway
D2 = Dual 2-lane carriageway
D3 = Dual 3-lane carriageway
D4 = Dual 4-lane carriageway
Estimated works costs are exclusive of VAT

TABLE 4:   NATIONAL TRUNK ROAD SCHEMES REVISED SINCE 24 APRIL 1987

M3	Widening Eastbound Carriageway Between Junctions 2 - 3, Surrey	Extended to cover widening both carriageways between Junctions 2 & 4, Surrey and Hampshire
M4	Free Flow Links Junction 8/9, Berkshire	Incorporated into M4 Widening between M25 Interchange & Junction 8/9
A1	Dishforth -- Scotch Corner Carriageway and Junction Improvements, N. Yorkshire	Split into A1 Leeming -- Scotch Corner Improvements and Dishforth -- Leeming Improvements Phase 2, N. Yorkshire
A11	Roudham Heath -- Snetterton, Norfolk	Extended to Roudham Heath -- Attleborough, Norfolk
A11	Thetford Bypass, Norfolk	To be dualled throughout
A11	West of Elveden Improvement, Suffolk	Superseded by A11 Fiveways Roundabout -- Bridgham Heath, Suffolk, Norfolk
A12	Farnham/Stratford St. Andrew Bypass, Suffolk	Superseded by A12 Wickham Market -- Saxmundham Bypass, Suffolk
A13	Cotton Street/Blackwall Tunnel Junction Improvement, LB Tower Hamlets	Scheme enlarged to include spur from northbound Blackwall Tunnel to Isle of Dogs
A27	Arundel Bypass, W. Sussex	Revised to exclude Crossbush Bypass, which is proceeding as a separate scheme
A30	Honiton to Exeter Improvement, Devon	Extended to include improvement of existing dual carriageway between Ironbridge and Honiton
A45	Flore Bypass, Northamptonshire	Superseded by Weedon, Flore and Upper Heyford Bypass
A45	St. Neots Bypass -- Croxton Crossroads, Cambridgeshire	Superseded by A45 Eaton Socon (A1) -- Hardwick Improvement
A46	Pennsylvania -- North of Field Lane Improvement, Avon	Extended to A46 Pennsylvania -- M4 (Tormarton) Improvement, Avon
A46	Bath (Upper Swainswick) -- A420, Avon	Extended to A46 Upper Swainswick -- Pennsylvania, Avon
A52	Basford / Hough Bypass, Cheshire	Extended and renumbered to A500 Basford -- Hough -- Shavington Bypass
A59	Burscough and Rufford Bypass, Lancashire	Superseded by A59 Ormskirk -- Walmer Bridge Improvement, Lancashire
A66	Temple Sowerby Bypass, Cumbria	Extended to include Improvement to Winderwath
A69	Warwick Bridge Bypass, Cumbria	Scheme under review
A259	Rye Improvement, E. Sussex	Scheme under review
A259	Winchelsea Bypass, E. Sussex	Scheme under review
A261	M20 -- A259 Hythe Improvement, Kent	Renamed A259 Dymchurch -- M20 (Junction 11), Kent
A419	Latton Bypass, Wiltshire	Extended to Wiltshire/Gloucestershire boundary
A419	Stratton Bypass, Gloucestershire	Extended to include bypass of Cirencester
A419	Stratton -- Birdlip, Gloucestershire	Extended to Crickley Hill, Gloucestershire
A428	Great Barford Bypass, Bedfordshire	Superseded by Great Barford Bypass and Extension to A1, Bedfordshire

TABLE 4:   NATIONAL TRUNK ROAD SCHEMES
REVISED SINCE 24 APRIL 1987

A438	West of Ashchurch -- A435, Gloucestershire	Superseded by A435/A438 South of Evesham -- M5 Improvement
A556	M56 (J7) -- M6 (J19) Improvement, Cheshire	Incorporated into Greater Manchester Western and Northern Relief Road
A590	Swarthmoor Bypass, Cumbria	Superseded by A590 Ulverston -- Dalton Bypass, Cumbria
A595	Howgate -- Hayes Castle Improvement, Cumbria	Superseded by A595 Parton -- Lillyhall Improvement, Cumbria
A596/A66	Workington Bypasses, Cumbria	Revised and shortened to A66 Stainburn and Great Clifton Bypass, Cumbria
A696	Belsay Bypass, Northumberland	Withdrawn) Need for schemes to be) reviewed after opening of
A696	Otterburn Bypass, Northumberland	Withdrawn) Newcastle Western Bypass

TABLE 5: LOCAL AUTHORITY SCHEMES APPROVED FOR CENTRAL GOVERNMENT GRANT UNDER S272 OF THE HIGHWAYS ACT 1980 AT 1 JANUARY 1990

	Standard	Estimated Total Cost (£million) *	Approximate Length (Miles)	Level of Grant; Progress
A15 Brigg and Redbourne Bypass, Humberside	S	7.4	5.0	100% Opened December 1989
A120 Stansted -- Braintree, Essex	D2	38.0	14.7	100% In Preparation
A418 Leighton Linslade Bypass, Bedfordshire	S	16.6	6.6	100% Tenders Invited Autumn 1989
(A696) Callerton Lane Link, Northumberland	S	1.2	1.0	85% In Preparation
Black Country Spine Road, Walsall MB, Wolverhampton MB, Sandwell MB	D2	126.2	4.4	100% In Preparation

* Costs shown for schemes under construction are at current prices; for schemes in preparation costs are at November 1987 prices.

Printed in the United Kingdom for HMSO.
Dd.292751, 5/90, C30, 3385/4, 5673, 93669.